CHINESE FOOD FINDER
THE BAY AREA
and San Francisco

S0-BDP-101

CARL CHU
Andrea Rademan, Contributing Editor

Chinese Food Finder – The Bay Area and San Francisco
A Guide to Chinese Regional Cuisines

By Carl Chu

Published by
Crossbridge Publishing Company
Box 3555, Manhattan Beach, California 90266
United States of America

Visit our website: http://www.crossbridgepublishing.com

ISBN: 1-932296-05-0
Library of Congress Control Number: 2004096187
First Edition

Printed in Taiwan

Disclaimer:

Restaurants come and go. And they happen all the time.
Although every effort is made to provide the most up-to-
date information, any error or omission in this book is wholly
unintentional. Both the author and publisher assume no
liability for the reader's loss, injury, or inconvenience resulting
from using information contained herein.

TABLE OF CONTENTS

PREFACE

When I published the first version of Chinese Food Finder: Los Angeles, reviewers acclaimed it for demystifying the daunting behemoth that is the Chinese menu. People tell me that the guide helped them unlock the secrets of where to go and what to order. That was comforting for me to hear: for a long time, I had been mystified about Chinese food myself.

Even though I grew up with a mixed northern Chinese/Taiwanese heritage, I did not encounter the full range of China's culinary landscape until sometime over the past 15 years. That was when a host of regional restaurants began sprouting in suburban San Gabriel Valley, here in Los Angeles where I have lived most of my life. Many of those encounters profoundly changed my perspectives. China is such a huge and diverse country that a Chinese from a different region often has conflicting notions about particular dishes. Is chow mein pan-fried or stir-fried noodles? Should Kungpao chicken contain green peppers? There may even be disagreement over whether dim sum is breakfast or lunch. Immersed in L.A.'s melting pot, diverse with different groups of Chinese, these questions often open the way to heated dialogue.

I went in search of the essence of Chinese food: exploring the cultural and historical contexts that make each regional cuisine so different, and eating around a wide swath of L.A. for glimpses of the regional flavor. My experiences eventually laid the foundations for the "Finder."

From my subsequent travels – to New York, San Francisco, Vancouver, and other cities with large Chinese populations – it became clear that North America is in the middle of a Chinese culinary revolution. Dining Chinese in the Bay Area was quite an interesting experience. The Chinese population is spread so evenly throughout the region that Chinese restaurants are nearly everywhere you go. In an older community like Mountain View, the pickings tend to stay with traditional takeouts. In the brand new strip malls of Milpitas, mainland home-cooking grub shares space next door to posh Hongkong-style seafood. And hardly anyone speaks of Chinatown as the purveyor of serious Chinese food anymore, even though lots of very good food still exists there.

This book reflects my painstaking approach in cataloguing the Bay Area's Chinese restaurants. I start by breaking down each restaurant into a regional category. Then I go further to describe the characteristics of each style. Typical dishes and the restaurants that are emblematic of that regional style are mentioned at the end. I created the "Finder" not only to open new vistas into the Bay Area's Chinese food scene, I wanted to introduce Chinese culinary culture to anyone interested in learning more about this fascinating tradition.

A NOTE ON DISH DESCRIPTIONS

To help overcome the Chinese-English language gap on most menus, I have used colloquial names for many dishes mentioned in this book. Translating colloquial names is problematic, because no two restaurants use the same descriptions. There are also many dubious translations. For instance, the famous Sichuan dish "Mapo tofu" translates literally as "Pockmark-face lady's tofu." But I have seen in different places "Sichuan-style Tofu," "Tofu in Hot Sauce," and a rather curious "Hot Grandma's Bean Curd." Although the Chinese are fond of these colloquial names, which are often witty and anecdotal, they seldom relate to the dish's appearance or taste. For Americans, this contributes partly to the frustration of Chinese dining.

I have tried to maintain the integrity of Chinese colloquial names whenever possible, mentioning either their Mandarin pronunciations, or literal translations. They are always followed by detailed descriptions, which not only explain the main characteristics of the dishes, but may also reveal interesting facts about them. This way, they also help in enhancing your Chinese food experience.

On the other hand, most Chinese dishes have simple descriptive names like "Flash-fried lamb with scallions," which merely list the ingredients. I have simply translated these names into English. Note that some dishes, such as "Water-boiled beef," are translated literally from the Chinese, while others, such as "Dongbo pork," are in phonetic form.

To use this book when ordering at a restaurant, you can attempt the Mandarin pronunciations, or point to the Chinese characters. Otherwise, try hand gestures (and your imagination) to describe the dish to the staff.

THE CHINESE IN AMERICA

The Guangdong people (Cantonese) were the first Chinese immigrants in America, arriving in the U.S. during the heady days of the California Gold Rush. More were recruited to work on the western half of the Transcontinental Railroad in 1864. Mostly men, they came from areas surrounding the city of Guangzhou (Canton) in Guangdong province. Thus, they were commonly referred to as the "Cantonese."

Although Guangdong province accounted for merely eight percent of China's population, for well over a century Guangdong immigrants made up nearly all the Chinese overseas. Immigration from other parts of China never materialized, because the Qing government barred all Chinese from overseas travel. Guangdong was the exception because of the British: the Crown's naval presence in the Pearl River Delta stemmed Beijing's power to exercise much control down there. This led to waves of law-defying expatriation, leading to, among other things, the common misperception that Guangdong cuisine represented that of all of China.

It was only after 1965, after the repeal of a series of anti-Chinese legislation, that Chinese from other regions began arriving in the U.S. in large numbers. First came the Hongkongers and Taiwanese, many of whom were wealthy professionals escaping the political uncertainties hovering over the Cold War. Others came virtually destitute. Whatever the circumstances, this second wave of Chinese immigrants arrived with a singular vision: they were willing to leave everything behind in order to pursue their American Dreams.

In 1978, three years after the end of the Vietnam War, many ethnic Chinese in Vietnam were forced to flee because of ethnic persecution. They were mainly Chaozhou people (Chiu Chow, or Teochew) who originally migrated to Southeast Asia during the 1850s. Through the first half of the 1980s, hundreds of thousands of these Vietnamese Boat

People took to the seas. About half perished at sea; those who survived the ordeal settled primarily in Los Angeles and Houston. Some also found their ways to the Bay Area.

Also in the 1980s, with the opening of mainland China, a more diversified class of people from Beijing, Shanghai, Sichuan, and other parts of China began arriving. Their numbers continue to increase today, and are changing the face of Chinese communities throughout America: Mandarin is replacing Cantonese as the *lingua franca* of Chinatown, and charsui pork must now share the spotlight with dongbo pork on the menu. Changes are happening quickly, and they are bound to bring about interesting microcosms of the Chinese right into our backyards.

THE CHINESE IN THE BAY AREA

The first Chinese workers had already arrived in Honolulu by 1831, so it was not for nearly twenty years before San Francisco saw its first Chinese immigrant wave. The Gold Rush of 1849 brought many Chinese men seeking fortune – just like the white men who came overland from the East. The Chinese did not bring their families with them, because they desired to return quickly to their ancestral Guangdong homes once they struck rich.

They soon found obstacles in their ventures, however. A series of anti-Chinese laws drove them out of the prospecting business altogether. Many went home, but those who stayed turned to farming and the restaurant business. Thus, for the first time America got its taste of Chinese food, Guangdong-style.

The second wave of Chinese immigrants arrived as laborers recruited for the Transcontinental Railroad. Also mainly men, and also from Guangdong province – particularly Taishan (Toishan) prefecture near the Pearl River Delta, these Chinese created San Francisco's Chinatown, the first in the continental United States.

Chinatown was mainly a bachelor's society through the first half of the twentieth century. Strict (and racist, mostly) laws prohibited Chinese women from entering the U.S., even to visit their husbands who had already settled here. In San Francisco Chinatown, men outnumbered women 700 to 1. Vices and crime festered as a matter of normalcy, as prostitution, gambling, and opium dens filled every crevice in the neighborhood. Gang-style tong wars broke out among rivaling factions in the 1910s, starting a long period of intra-Chinese fighting that ended only after the Second World War. In other words, for a long time Chinatown was a place where people avoided going.

The liberalization of U.S. immigration policies in 1965 profoundly changed the Chinese community in the Bay Area. The arrival of women brought about families to Chinatown, and replaced brothels and gambling halls with a new industry: Chinese restaurants. And as the cap on the number of Chinese immigrants was removed, the Chinese began pouring in from Taiwan and Hongkong. This time, the new immigrants found little affinity with the Guangdong people in Chinatown, so they settled elsewhere. Many were also wealthy when they arrived, so they could afford to live in the suburbs, like the Richmond District or Mountain View farther away.

In the 1970s, the computer revolution brought many skilled scientists and technicians to the Silicon Valley. This group also included many Chinese entrepreneurs. It is in the South Bay where much of the colorful Chinese food scene is found today. The strip malls of Cupertino, Fremont, and Milpitas have emerged as supreme venues for some of the most exciting Chinese food around, transcending the old chop suey and chow mein stereotypes with a brand new vocabulary for eating Chinese: wowotou, xiaolongbao, and herbal hotpots.

Today, more Chinese continue to arrive, especially from mainland China. Complex as the Chinese society actually is, their presence has brought about wholly different sensitivities toward everything the Chinese community thinks and does. Who is a more influential writer, Lu Xun or Amy Tan? How do you steam fish, with ginger and scallions or lots of fermented soybeans? Old perceptions of the Chinese do not apply anymore, and in time the complexion of the Chinese in the Bay Area will change again in profound and heretofore unexpected ways.

CHINESE FOOD AND DRINK

Although written proof of Chinese cooking has existed for more than 2,000 years, most of today's regional Chinese cuisines are less than 600 years old. Within this span of time, China experienced everything from famine to foreign domination. The Manchus, a non-Han minority, established the Qing Dynasty (1644-1911). During the nineteenth and mid-twentieth centuries, Western imperialists carved out various parts of China under their governance. Further, wars with Britain, Japan, and its own people dealt hardship and misery that brought about the near extinction of this once invincible nation.

Amid so much change and trauma, Chinese cooking traditions evolved by incorporating various outside influences. Yet it remains largely "Chinese" in substance and style. It is this resilience – one that draws from both Chinese and foreign ideas, while steadfastly maintaining its distinct identity – that makes Chinese food one of the most respected and acclaimed culinary traditions in the world.

TEA DRINKING IN CHINESE FOOD

Tea drinking is inseparable from Chinese culture, and it is the mother's milk that nurtures the civilization. The Chinese drink tea on any occasion: with friends, at work, on the airplane, et cetera. For the most part, Chinese tea is of no extraordinary quality. It is, to many Chinese, just something to drink instead of plain boiled water. Many people visiting China are surprised to see the Chinese drinking their teas out of mason jars and tannin-stained glasses. But this is just a common beverage for common people after all. It also goes to show how prevalent and unspectacular tea drinking is in China.

China is one of several great producers of teas in the world, ranking second after India in the tonnage of teas exported. The history of tea cultivation in China extends well before Christ's time, but its development has been slow and sporadic over the centuries. Today, generally better quality teas are grown in India and Taiwan, even though they only started tea cultivation no more than 200 years ago.

The teas of the world fall into one of three general categories: black teas (fully oxidized), oolong teas (partially oxidized), and green teas (unoxidized). India and Sri Lanka (Ceylon) are famous for their black teas. Taiwan is renowned for world-class oolongs. Japan is known for its unique green teas. Only China produces all three categories of teas. They vary from the black Keemun, the oolong Ti Kuan Yin, and the green Longjing.

The Teas of China

Black (fully oxidized) Teas

The teas popularized by the English and the West are black teas. Tealeaves are allowed to oxidize fully in the drying and production processes, creating deep, red colors and rich, intense flavors in the brewed tea. For that matter, the Chinese call these "red" teas.

Westerners drink their black teas in a considerably different manner than the Chinese. Westerners prefer a great deal of blending to create multitudes of flavors in the tea. Often, tealeaves from India, Sri Lanka, and China are selected together to create such proprietary names as "Earl Grey," "Irish Breakfast," and even Lipton's perennially consistent tea bags. Westerners also prefer adding lemon or milk to control the tea's bitterness and astringency.

The Chinese prefer drinking varietal black teas. That is, black teas are unblended and unembellished in any way. Keemun, Pu-er, and Yunnan are major examples of Chinese black varietals. Occasionally the teas are infused with herbal or fruit flavors to control their intensity. The Chinese never drink their teas with lemon or milk, unless the teas are served in western-style coffeeshops, or as the trendy "Boba Tea."

Keemun
祁門

Grown in the Qimen (Keemun) district of Anhui province, Keemun is the most famous black tea from China. Although its quality is overshadowed by the black teas from India, like Assam and Darjeeling, Keemun has a sweet flavor that is versatile for blending with other herbs or varietals. For that reason, most of the Keemun production is blended in one form or another. The best quality Keemun can sometimes be drunk on its own merit.

Yunnan
雲南

This tea from the namesake southwestern province has floral scents and a rich, malty flavor. Yunnan is often blended with other black teas, creating such famous names as Harrod's (a London department store) proprietary "Assam and Yunnan" tea. Even when it is drunk on its own, Yunnan is best served with milk to tame its high tannin content.

Lapsang Souchong
正山小種

The Gewürztraminer of teas is one that inspires the most polemical emotions in people. Lapsang Souchong's dark, woodsy, and smoky flavors are qualities that people either love or hate, with little middle ground in between. According to legend, "Lapsang" was discovered completely by accident. Short on time to dry the tealeaves, tea producers heated them over burning pine and cedar woods. In the process, they discovered that the distinctive scents and flavors of the woods were fully infused into the tea. Today, Lapsang Souchong is grown mainly in Fujian province.

Pu-er
普洱

A cheap and mediocre tea from Yunnan province, Pu-er is popular only with the Guangdong people. The rest of China avoids it like Dracula to sunlight. Pu-er is a so-called "110%-oxidized" tea: water is reintroduced to the dry, fully-oxidized leaves for a second round of oxidation. The result is a very dark tea of reddish-brown color. It has earthy flavors with unremarkable undertones. A sheer film of natural oils usually appears at the top, giving the brewed tea an unappealing appearance. The love of the Guangdong people for Pu-er is unshakable, and its association with dim sum/yum cha is forever etched in the commandments of Chinese food culture. Besides, Pu-er purportedly has grease-cutting qualities that facilitate better digestion of fatty dim sum, justifying its central role as the cha in yum cha.

Brick Tea
茶磚

Poor quality Pu-er tea is pressed into bricks for the non-Han hinterlands of northwestern- and southwestern China, as well as Tibet and Mongolia. For one, the Mongolian way of drinking tea is unlike anything both the eastern- and western cultures are familiar with. The tea brick is first smashed into pieces, and then tossed into a boiling pot of water along with yak butter and salt. The concoction is served hot, with tealeaves and floating pieces of fat altogether gulped down for an eye-opening drink.

Oolong (partially oxidized) Teas

Partially oxidized teas are golden-brown in color, with mild flavors that fall between those of black and green teas. However, oolongs have extra dimensions that are quite complex, giving them the world's attention that they deserve. Because of oolong's delicate flavors, much of it, except for the ordinary grades, are left without any blending, flavoring, or scenting. Oolongs should be steeped several times so that the drinker can experience the different dimensions of the tea in each steeping. Though complex, the dimensions are often subtle and are easily conquered by even milk. Therefore, oolongs are better drunk without any embellishments.

The best oolongs are grown in central Taiwan, in 3,000-foot-plus elevations near the Tropic of Cancer. These areas are constantly shrouded in cool mists, which is the ideal condition for oolongs. Because of the island's small size and limited production, these oolongs are also some of the world's most expensive teas.

Tung Ting Oolong
凍頂烏龍

Meaning "Frosted Summit," this specialty oolong is the most famous from Taiwan. Originally grown only on the steep slopes of Tung Ting Shan (Frosted Summit Mountain) in Nantou prefecture, producers recently began growing Tung Ting throughout the mountainous regions of central Taiwan. Still, they barely produce enough to meet the demand worldwide. The light, fruity, and flowery scents of Tung Ting are complemented by a long-lasting, sweet aftertaste. Additionally, the brewed tea has a sparkling body that gives off a slight, refreshing effervescence when sipped.

Ti Kuan Yin
鐵觀音

Grown in Fujian province, on the mainland side of the Taiwan Strait, Ti Kuan Yin is the forebear of Taiwan's oolong crop. Ti Kuan Yin, or "Iron Goddess of Mercy," is generally darker than Taiwanese oolongs. It undergoes fifty- to seventy percent oxidation, compared to forty percent for Taiwanese oolongs. While most of the Ti Kuan Yins are only of moderate quality, some of the best have dimensions similar to Tung Ting, which allow producers to justifiably command prices upwards of $200 per pound.

Pouchong
包種

The foothills surrounding Taipei city proper, in northern Taiwan, are dotted with small tea plantations that produce the only Pouchongs in the world. Pouchong, which is only ten percent oxidized, is lighter in flavor than all other oolongs. Likewise, the milder dimensions are not nearly as complex. Pouchong can be found both on its own as an ordinary varietal, or scented into flavored teas. Most Taiwanese productions of jasmine tea are made from Pouchong as well.

GREEN (UNOXIDIZED) TEAS

When tealeaves are steamed, dried, and roasted without allowing them to undergo any oxidation, the end product is green tea, which retains most of the tea's natural characteristics: flowery aromas, mellow flavors, and subtle hints of the earth. Although green tea is generally associated with Japanese tea culture, it is the primary type of tea that the Chinese drink.

China grows several famous varieties of green teas. Additionally, there are "white teas" that are merely dried tealeaves without the customary steaming and roasting processes. White tea has a pure, natural taste without the added complexities derived from heating green teas.

Longjing
龍井

Sometimes called "Dragon Well," the most famous green tea from China is grown in Zhejiang province, in the mountains surrounding West Lake outside the city of Hangzhou. Longjing tealeaves are hand-rolled into needle-like shapes, and through the roasting process they attain a rich, nutty flavor. This is an unusual flavor for green teas, which may suggest why Longjing tealeaves are a vital cooking ingredient in Jiangzhe cuisine. Longjing is featured

THE UNSAID CADENCE OF FINGER-TAPPING

Keep a sharp eye out next time when having dim sum/yum cha, or any kind of Chinese food for that matter. You may notice that when someone pours tea for their friend, they respond by tapping their fingers next to the teacup. Why?

One story says the practice originated with a Qing Dynasty emperor, who once traveled to southern China to survey his subjects. Not wanting to be noticed, he wore commoner's clothes and refrained from speaking in public. His court attire and northern dialect would have instantly revealed him as a nobleman. One evening, while dining in a country inn, the emperor's servant poured him tea. Keeping to his silent bit, the emperor tapped his fingers on the table as a sign of gratitude. From then on, the emperor and his servant agreed that tapping fingers would be his way of expressing thanks.

Another story attributes this *digital reflex* to the sparing emotions of the Guangdong people. Renowned for their loud and nonstop chatter, many found it belaboring to stop mid-sentence to say a "*thank you*." So they tapped their fingers instead, while the conversation at hand continued uninterrupted. As time went by, finger-tapping became a commonly accepted way of acknowledging another's kindness. But it remains a practice reserved for tea (i.e. don't do it at Black Jack).

Whatever the real story is, responding to someone's *pu-er*-pouring courtesy by gently tapping two or three fingers instantly exposes you as an insider to Chinese food etiquette, and also as someone who cherishes the unsaid bond of kinship between friends.

in a famous dish called, appropriately enough, "Shrimp Stir-fried with Longjing Tealeaves."

Gunpowder Tea

Another green tea from Zhejiang province, gunpowder tea gets its name from the shape of the finished tealeaves, which are rolled into grayish-green pellets resembling old-fashioned gunpowder. These teas are usually of low or moderate quality, possessing earthy and unassuming flavors that are more suited for ordinary, everyday drinking than for special occasions and entertaining.

Huangshan Maofeng
黃山毛峰

This green tea, often simply called "Maofeng," comes from the scenic Yellow Mountains (Huangshan) of southern Anhui province. Maofeng is quite rare outside China, because its quality is still inconsistent after decades of austere communist rule. The surroundings of Huangshan, with its mist-shrouded hills and consistently moist conditions, make ideal growing conditions for this tea, making it a prime candidate as a world-class tea in the future.

Pi Lo Chun
碧螺春

A very rare green tea from China, Pi Lo Chun (pinyin: Biluochun) is of considerably higher quality than all other Chinese green teas. Grown in the mountains near Suzhou, arguably China's most scenic city, the bushes of Pi Lo Chun are planted next to apricot, peach, plum, and mandarin orange trees to allow the leaves to absorb sublime hints of these fruits. Tealeaves are handpicked only in the spring, when they are just beginning to bud. During the drying process, the leaves are rolled into small, snail shell-like pellets before roasting. The tea was so enamored by a 17th century Qing emperor that he gave it its poetic name, which means "A Spring of Green Snails."

White Down Silver Needles
白毫銀針

This is a white tea that, like all other white teas of

China, is grown in Fujian province. The tealeaves are picked only in April, just before the first buds are about to open. The amount of silvery fuzz on the underside of the leaves gives the tea its name. When brewed, white tea has a pale, yellow color with a clean, mellow flavor. White Down Silver Needles is a "showpiece" tea, meaning that it should be served in a glass teapot or cup, so that the drinker can appreciate the appearance of the tealeaves.

Green Peony
綠牡丹

Also a showpiece tea, green peony is more spectacular for its appearance than for the taste. It is nevertheless a visually stunning example of China's broad variety of teas. Produced in Anhui province, Green Peony is made by tying whole, unbroken, and unoxidized tealeaves into a compact bundle, then pressed into a flat disk before drying and roasting. When the disk is steeped, it "blooms" into a flower-like shape resembling a peony flower. As it is meant to make an impression upon the drinker, Green Peony should also be served in a glass teapot or cup.

HERBAL AND FLAVORED TEAS

Coffee producers make flavored coffees from ordinary coffee beans that have no particularly attractive qualities. Tea producers do the same, by infusing low quality tealeaves with the scents of herbs, flowers, or fruits to boost their marketing value. Popular herbal teas include the flavors of chamomile, chrysanthemum, ginger, gingko, ginseng, hibiscus, jasmine, lychee, and guava.

Jasmine Tea
香片

Jasmine is the most popular of the flavored teas from China. Jasmine flower petals are layered on top of green tealeaves during the drying process, allowing the floral fragrances to be absorbed. Taiwanese jasmine uses locally grown Pouchong, which are minimally oxidized for a slightly richer flavor than other green tea-based jasmines. Low and moderate quality jasmine will contain some flower petals in the finished product. The best contains only the scented tealeaves. One such example is "Pearl

Jasmine," in which the leaves are scented numerous times to produce a concentrated fragrance, and rolled into pellet-shaped rounds. Sometimes, Pearl Jasmine uses rare teas such as White Down Silver Needles as its base.

Boba Tea
波霸茶

The name "Boba Tea" has risen from total obscurity fifteen years ago to a food fad on the verge of worldwide fame. Also called "Bubble" or "Pearl" tea, it can be found in coffeeshops and beverage kiosks throughout North America, sustaining the current and future generations of mall rats with plenty of sugar and starch.

Boba tea is the combination of boba (chewy starch balls made from yams) with iced tea. People often mistake boba as tapioca. In reality, yam starch gives boba its dark brown color. The chewiness, resembling gummy candy, is something the Taiwanese describe as "Q." They are quite crazy about it. The tea part of Boba tea is any ordinary black tea, sweetened with condensed milk and non-dairy creamer. All that is shaken with crushed ice and slurped up with a large colorful straw.

| 祁門功夫紅茶 3601 | 珍品明前龍井 3622 | 三杯香綠茶 |
| Imperial Keemun Black 4oz | Lungching Premium 4oz | Triple-Cup Extra Green |

| 門全葉紅茶 3301 | 西湖龍井綠茶 3322 | 黃山翠尖綠茶 |
| un Full Leaf Black 8.8oz | Lungching Green 8.8oz | Huang Mtn. Tippy Green |

| 真紅紅茶 3366 | 西湖龍井綠茶 3922 | 雨前毛峰綠茶 36 |
| Gold Tip Black 8.8oz | Dragonwell Lungching 8oz | Before Rain Tippy Green 2.5 |

| 江紅茶 3903 | 碧螺春綠茶 3621 | 江南毛峰綠茶 39 |
| Black 8oz | Pilochun Spiral Green 4oz | Mao Feng Green |

| 茶 3311 | 四川蒙頂綠茶 3626 | 日式玄米綠茶 33 |
| 8.8oz | Sichuan Meng Ding Green 4oz | Genmaicha Green 8.8 |

| 3305 | 黃山毛峰綠茶 3628 | 日本煎茶(一番) 33 |
| 8.8oz | Huang Mtn. Maofeng 2oz | Japanese Sencha Green 8.8 |

WHERE TO BUY TEA IN THE BAY AREA

There are a few specialty tea shops selling terrific Chinese teas, but you don't necessarily have to search out the most obscure of places in order to get the best. The flourishing transpacific trade has made Chinese teas readily available around town, from supermarkets to wholesale outlets. Here are a few consistent and mainstream purveyors.

Peet's Tea & Coffee

Don't be fooled by the Starbucks-like aura of this chain. The teas are meticulously chosen from estates throughout the world, including some of the more obscure selections from China. Among the noteworthy Chinese teas in Peet's product line are Green Peony and Jasmine Downy Pearls. A handy tea guide is available in-store to help you decide among the assortments. The staff are especially helpful with suggestions.

There are many locations throughout the Bay Area.

Website: http://www.peets.com

Ten Ren Co.
天仁茗茶

Ten Ren is best known for its Tung Ting Oolong. There are also Puchongs from Ten Ren's estates outside Taipei. Other green and black teas are imported from China, but they often suffer from inconsistent quality because Ten Ren doesn't actually grow these teas themselves.

10881 N. Wolfe Rd., Cupertino
408.873.2038

1732 N. Milpitas Blvd., Milpitas
408.946.1118

39115 Cedar Blvd., Newark
510.713.9588

3288 Pierce St., #C161, Richmond
510.526.3989

949 Grant Ave., Chinatown
415.362.0656

Website: http://www.tenren.com

Imperial Tea Court
裕隆茶莊

Both a teahouse and a teashop, you can sit down and enjoy a nice cup of tea while the rest of the world busies itself away. You can sit for hours just soaking in the ambience alone. The selection of teas includes many rare types from China and Taiwan.

1411 Powell St., Chinatown
415.788.6080
11.00 - 18.30, closed Tuesdays

Ferry Building, San Francisco
415.544.9830
10.00 - 18.00, closed Mondays

101 Tea Plantation
101 茶園

The family-owned tea grower/ wholesaler imports many prize-worthy oolongs directly from its estates in Nantou prefecture of central Taiwan. A limited selection of black and green teas is also available, but it's oolong that's boss here.

46859 Warm Springs Blvd., Fremont
510.623.9606

REGIONAL STYLES OF CHINA

When we speak of Chinese Food, we are really referring to the cooking of the Hans – the ethnic majority that make up over ninety percent of China's population. This is true even though the Hans live only in about half of China's landmass. Despite the existence of 55 minority groups, Chinese regional cuisines represent only Han culture, and share very little similarity with the traditions of other minorities.

Chinese food consists of four major styles: Southern, Northern, Western, and Eastern. Depending on who you ask though, there can be as many variations to these styles as there are Kamehameha Roads in Hawaii, with every village, city, and province offering some claim to their own specialties. But generally, all of the Han cooking styles can be categorized into these groups.

Socially, regional differences in China are more pronounced than they are in the U.S. The northern dialect (Mandarin) is incomprehensible to a Guangdong (Cantonese) speaker – and vice versa. The dialect of Shanghai people in the east is incomprehensible to the people of Sichuan in the west. Regional variations of Chinese cuisine are as diverse as the Hans people themselves.

And don't count on your Chinese friends to help you sort through these differences. Most Chinese are only familiar with their own regional cuisines, and are likely to approach other cooking styles with equal cluelessness as you.

SOUTHERN CHINA

The cuisine of southern China is represented by the Guangdong style of cooking. Because of the long-time dominance of Guangdong immigrants abroad, it is often mistaken simply as "Chinese food." In actuality, Guangdong cuisine is the youngest of China's four classic regional styles, and it is not a particularly sophisticated style of cooking.

Southern Chinese cooking is in essence Chinese food for beginners. Dishes are uncomplicated – using light, sweet, and tepid sauces over quickly stir-fried foods. Other dishes employ basic, straightforward steps like steaming and boiling. This characteristic works especially well with seafood, paving the way for the splendors of Hongkong-style seafood, and also Chaozhou cuisine that infuses unmistakable touches of Southeast Asia with traditional Chinese cookery. Even dim sum has roots with extraordinarily humble beginnings. Other styles, such as Fujian, Hakka, and Hunan, are not very well known outside China, and have a minor presence in the Bay Area.

GUANGDONG CUISINE

During the past 200 years Guangdong (Cantonese) cuisine emerged from its nondescript, peasant roots to become a distinct cooking style. Before then, the only recognized Chinese regional styles were northern (Shandong), eastern (Jiangzhe), and western (Sichuan).

The development of Guangdong cuisine really took off after 1842, when the British defeated China in the First Opium War. Faced with a foreign presence, the local cooking style adapted many heretofore unfamiliar ingredients, such as tomatoes ("foreigner's eggplant"), watercress ("European vegetable"), and curry from India. These are rarely found in the cuisines of other regions. There is also more deep-frying, a western cooking technique.

Despite these outside influences, Guangdong cuisine is basically simple, country-style cooking. Dishes are simple and easy to prepare. Rapid stir-frying is the primary cooking method; the short cooking times preserve the natural flavors and textures of the ingredients. There is little of the intricate knifework, technique, and interplay of ingredients that are inherent in other regional styles. Overall, Guangdong cooking features light and fruity flavors, and starchy sauces that appeal to western palates. It is less popular with the Chinese (except the Guangdong people of course), and is commonly dismissed as "flavorless" in deference to heavier, more complex flavors.

To a degree, Guangdong cooking owes its popularity in America to the fact that this was virtually the only Chinese food available for more than 100 years. In fact, dishes such as orange-flavor chicken, broccoli beef, and egg fu-yung – all based on the classic Guangdong cooking style – can justifiably be called American food.

OF RICE AND MEIN: GUANGDONG COOKERY

Although Guangdong has a few dishes that are well-known throughout China, this style of cookery is eminently practical. The thickness of a typical Guangdong menu is indicative of the immense number of dishes native to this region, most of which consist of combinations of meats and vegetables. On the menu, dishes are usually grouped into categories like "Rice," "Noodles," and "Earthenware Hotpots."

BARBECUE

The barbecue shop is a unique and popular feature of Guangdong-style restaurants. Shop windows are stocked with roast ducks, boiled chickens, sides of suckling pig, and *charsui* pork. Most barbecue shops are located adjacent to the restaurant dining room, and serve both dine-in and takeout customers. Many barbecue items are used in Guangdong home cooking, so people often drop by as part of their daily shopping agenda.

Roast Duck
粵式燒鴨

Unlike Beijing ducks, which have a distinctive crackly skin texture due to a complicated cooking technique (see page 94), the ducks in a barbecue shop are simply marinated in a brine of salt, sugar, and five-spice, then roasted over an open flame until golden brown. These ducks can be eaten with plum sauce as an appetizer, or they can be used as a flavoring ingredient in all kinds of stir-fries and soups.

Boiled Chicken
鹽水雞

In the Guangdong style, boiled chicken is left lightly undone, with a bit of red blood residue still in the bones. This way, the meat retains a slightly chewy texture. Chopped into bite-sized pieces, boiled chicken can be an appetizer or an entrée. A tray of minced ginger and scallions, marinated in oil, usually accompanies it as a dipping sauce.

Soy Sauce Chicken
豉油雞

Soy sauce chicken is prepared in the similar technique as the boiled chicken. The soy sauce in the cooking brine gives it a pale brown color and an altogether richer flavor. Eaten the same way as the boiled chicken, this is also accompanied by a dipping sauce of ginger and scallions.

Charsui ("barbecue") Pork
叉燒肉

An important ingredient in Guangdong home cooking, charsui pork is the benchmark by which all barbecue shops are judged. Charsui means "hooked roast," suggesting the technique of roasting. Sides of pork loin or ribs are marinated with salt, hoisin sauce, and honey, then placed on a hook over open flames. As a cooking ingredient, charsui pork is versatile for use in stir-fries and also as a filling for steamed baozi.

Roast Suckling Pig
燒乳豬

Suckling pigs are roasted until the skin is golden and crispy from head to tail. Traditionally, families raised pigs at home and reserved making this dish only for special occasions. Today, barbecue shops make this task all but unnecessary. It is available everyday and in small portions so it can be used to stir-fry seasonal greens, or put in all types of rice and noodle dishes.

RICE

Rice is an all-purpose starch in Chinese cooking. It is eaten plain of course, or used to make *fun*, vermicelli, and rice cakes. The most humble Chinese meal consists of a small amount of cooked vegetables eaten with a heaping mound of rice. Sometimes meats are included. These simple meals often show up on the Guangdong menu as a part of a larger, bewildering selection of dishes.

Chow Fun
炒粉

Fun is a broad, flat rice noodle. Chow fun is a stir-fry of fun with meats and vegetables. Although the name is similar to chow mein (see below), chow fun cannot be pan-fried because of its high moisture content. Many chow fun dishes demonstrate a Southeast Asian tilt in flavors. Satay beef chow fun is a very popular dish. So is chow fun with curry and tomatoes in the so-called "Singaporean-style."

Rice Vermicelli
米粉

Like chow fun, rice vermicelli is a stir-fried rice noodle dish. It is much thinner than fun, with thickness closer to angel hair pasta. The choice between the flat, broad fun and the thin, stringy vermicelli is purely a matter of personal preference. Alternative spellings for vermicelli, based on local dialects, include *mai fun*, *mee fun*, and *bee hon*. (In pinyin, it is *mifeng*.)

MIAN (NOODLES)

Rice is the primary staple in southern China, and wheat is the staple of the north. Noodles, a typical feature of the north, nevertheless play a supporting role in the Guangdong diet. Guangdong-style restaurants generally make passable but not stellar batches of noodles, with chow mein, lo mein, and yi-fu noodles being the most popular. Translations can sometimes be confusing: lo mein at one place may be called chow mein at another; and what the Guangdong people call chow mein has no equivalent in the takeout restaurants of main street America.

Chow Mein
炒麵

Chow mein is often incorrectly described as stir-fried noodles. In some places, chow mein is a stir-fry without any noodles at all. In authentic Guangdong cuisine, yolk-colored egg noodles are steamed, blanched, and fried in a shallow pan. Because chow mein is fried in a clump, the outside is crispy while the inside is soft, preferably al dente. A starchy sauce, such as seafood in a light broth, or a combination of tomatoes and beef, is slathered on top just before serving.

Lo Mein
撈麵

Guangdong-style lo mein is a noodle dish with the noodles culled out of the soup (lo means "culled"). The noodles are served dry with the meats and vegetables heaped on top. The soup is served separately as an accompanying "beverage." Lo mein is typically topped with barbecued meats, beef brisket, or even wontons.

Yi-fu Noodles
伊府麵

Commonly called yi mian, this noodle originated from Shandong province, the apex of Chinese noodle-making. These stringy, pale white noodles are made from flour, egg whites and oil, which give them a wriggly texture. Yi-fu noodles are mostly served in a soup. The only stir-fried yi-fu noodles is quite plain, with nothing more than chopped scallions. Alternative spellings include: yi mein, yee mein, and e-noodles.

Earthenware Hotpot
沙鍋

A distinctive Guangdong dish is the earthenware hotpot. Ingredients usually include a mix of seafood, meats, and tofu. Vegetables like Napa cabbage and cellophane noodles also frequent the pot. Everything is slowly simmered until it becomes a hearty stew. An especially popular one is a combination of pork spareribs and eggplant. Another one is fish head simmered with Napa cabbage. The hotpot, which doubles as the serving vessel, is brought directly from the stove to the table while the contents are still bubbling hot inside.

TYPICAL GUANGDONG STIR-FRIES

Many of the typical Guangdong-style stir-fries can be found in Chinese takeouts. These are the most recognizable dishes to Americans, using familiar meats and ingredients. Some Guangdong dishes are adaptations of other Chinese regional specialties, altered to suit the Guangdong palate which generally prefers light, mild, and uncomplicated flavors.

Beef-and-Broccoli
芥蘭牛肉

Not much more needs to be said about this takeout favorite. Broccoli is a European vegetable, brought to China in the 19th century. It is simply stir-fried with tender slices of beef, and flavored with oyster sauce. In authentic form, broccoli is replaced by gai lan, also called Chinese broccoli.

Beef Brisket in Tomato Sauce
蕃茄牛肉

Tomato, which the Chinese call "foreigner's eggplant," is not a common vegetable in Chinese cooking. Neither is beef, which is not as widely eaten as pork. The combination of tomatoes and beef gives this dish a western aura. In fact, a stew like this is often called "American-style." This dish is popularly served over plain rice or chow mein. Sometimes the stew alone is served as the main entrée.

Beef Flash-fried with Scallions
蔥爆(蒙古)牛肉

Often called Mongolian Beef, this dish is adapted from Islamic Chinese cuisine from northern China. As the name suggests, beef is stir-fried with scallions, with very little sauce. The alternative name – Mongolian beef – suggests the dish's origins from the north, adapted for Guangdong palates by using scallions instead of leeks, which appears more often in northern Chinese cooking.

Chicken with Cashews
腰果雞丁

Cashew nuts are indigenous to the Americas, so this dish suggests a multi-cultural dimension. Diced chicken is stir-fried in a light soy sauce with crunchy pieces of cashew nuts, making good use of contrasting textures and flavors.

Kungpao (Gongbao) Chicken
宮保雞丁

Kungpao chicken, in its familiar Americanized form, is an adaptation of an adaptation. This dish originally came from Guizhou province, near Sichuan, which is famous for hot and spicy foods. A milder, sweeter version was adapted to better suit the Guangdong palate. When kungpao traveled to the U.S., it got a second adaptation, this time with American ingredients such as bell peppers and yellow onions. Often the original requisites of chili peppers and peanuts are completely left out.

Pork Spareribs with Salt and Pepper
椒鹽排骨

This uncomplicated dish is very popular. Pork spareribs are deep-fried without any batter. A dish of salt and black pepper is provided on the side for dipping.

Sweet-and-sour pork
甜酸肉

Guangdong dishes use a lot of deep-frying, and prefer flavors that are sweet and fruity. Both characteristics can be found in sweet-and-sour pork. Pork pieces are battered and fried, then coated with a tart, fruity plum sauce. Chinese takeout restaurants usually use a reddish plum sauce bought in tubs from warehouses. Without food coloring, plum sauce is actually golden in color.

Stir-fried Squid in Shrimp Sauce
蝦醬鮮魷

Many people never grow acclimated to the pungency of shrimp sauce. More accurately, it is the pale-blue shrimp paste found in Asian supermarkets. The strong flavor is an acquired taste: earthy, salty, and definitively rustic. A little bit of it goes a long way. A dish like this often appears only on the Chinese-only menu, even though it is not an extraordinary dish by any stretch of the imagination.

Fried Rock Cod Fillet with Corn Sauce
粟米石班

Pieces of rock cod are battered and fried, then coated with a sauce made from canned cream of corn soup. Combining deep-frying with a mass-produced American product, this dish doesn't seem Chinese at all. Perhaps it isn't, but this illustrates the extent of foreign influences on the whole of Guangdong cuisine.

WHERE TO EAT GUANGDONG IN THE BAY AREA

Chinese food in Chinatown is still pretty much the same ol' Guangdong cuisine that has haunted it for over a century. The assessment may be unfair to a handful of places that buck the stereotype, but the overwhelming majority of Chinatown restaurants fit the same mold.

Elsewhere in the Bay Area, Guangdong restaurants thrive in older Chinese neighborhoods in Oakland and the Peninsula, but they diminish to a mere smattering in and around the Silicon Valley. Overall, the quality of Guangdong cuisine in the Bay Area is without a doubt the best in North America. It's not necessarily for the abundance of restaurants, but for the few adventurous types who challenge long-held traditions with refreshing takes on ingredients and techniques. These chefs have elevated Guangdong cuisine to a higher, more sophisticated level, and are taking it to an exciting future ahead.

Chueung Hing Restaurant
祥興燒臘小館

241-245 El Camino Real, Millbrae
650.652.3938
10.30 – 21.30

Mastercard, Visa

A large and well-stocked barbecue shelf beckons passersby on El Camino Real. It's just within the contrail range of SFO's runway 1L. Barbecue items include suckling pig, roast duck, soy sauce chicken, and Chaozhou-style master-cooked meats ("marinated assortment" on the menu). The rest is a consistent menu of Guangdong classics popular with locals for eating in or takeout.

New China Station B.B.Q.
新中國燒臘飯店

The crowded barbecue shop provides a reliable outlet for roast duck in this neck of the woods, which doesn't purvey as much Guangdong cuisine as its neighbors to the north. A busy dining room is actually attached next to it, dishing out all the chow mein, chow fun, and charsui you grew up to love. The earthenware hotpots ("clay pot") are quite fortifying, especially during winter.

1828 N. Milpitas Blvd., Milpitas
408.942.1686
10.30 – 21.30

Mastercard, Visa

Man Bo Duck Restaurant
萬寶鴨子樓

The house serves three types of ducks: "Peking" duck, smoked tea duck (adapted from the Sichuan style), and a "five spices crispy" duck. All are deep-fried so none are authentic. A handful of duck-themed dishes, like twice-cooked duck ("with Peking sauce"), pineapple duck, and duck salad constitutes the unique extent of this place. Other than that, it's a repeat bout of takeout classics common with other Chinese restaurants in this area.

360 Castro St., Mountain View
650.961.6635
11.00 – 00.00, until 01.00 on weekends

All credit cards

Yung Kee Restaurant
鏞記

You get consistent-quality rice, noodles, and stir-fries at this place, which is very popular with the locals. Chow mein is especially good here; you can have them in styles of: beef-and-tomato; scrambled eggs-with-shrimp; and lots more. Among the stir fries, stick with the steak cubes, cashew chicken, and the like.

888 Webster St., Oakland
510.839.2010
09.00 – 02.00, until 03.00 on weekends

Cash only

Daimo Chinese Restaurant
地茂館香港美食

This Hongkong-based chain is best known for its house-made noodles. You can have them in a soup, as lo mein, or as chow mein. The varieties are typical of any other Guangdong restaurant, but things are done a little different here. Try them with ostrich, pig knuckle, or even lobster. The ordinary stuff from the barbecue shelf (roast duck, sucking pig, soy sauce chicken) is also quite good.

3288-A Pierce St., Richmond
510.527.3888
09.00 – 03.00

Mastercard, Visa

R&G Lounge
嶺南小館

Situated at the edge of Chinatown, R&G is better positioned as the future of mainstream Chinese food. The décor is bright and cheery, but yet classy and understated. The food is smart and creative, like steak in XO sauce, and braised loofah melon with dried scallops. Chaozhou's master-cooked meats ("soya sauce" items) join Guangdong-style barbecues side-by-side in a variety of appetizers and main dishes. Come here for a lively diversion from the tired old Chinatown scene.

631 Kearny St., Chinatown

415.982.7877
11.00 – 21.30

All credit cards

Chef Jia's
喜福家

It's not anywhere near Hunan cuisine as it claims to be, but the food is very good. Dishes here transcend the takeout tradition with a higher level of dexterity in the making, and sophistication in substance. Try the chicken with string beans, prawns with yam, and beef with pinenuts. All are distant approximations to Hunan cooking with serious Guangdong sensitivities: hot and spicy, and bursting with fresh and natural flavors.

925 Kearny St., Chinatown
415.398.1626
11.30 – 22.00

Cash only

Ton Kiang
東江

The banner outside says Hakka cuisine, but the menu inside is all Guangdong – albeit with a lot of creativeness. Steamed catfish in black bean sauce, stir-fried okra with XO sauce, and stir-fried beef with basil all emerge from Guangdong traditions with strikingly different flavors. Together with a few actual Hakka dishes (see page 76) Ton Kiang offers up quite an unique dining experience.

5821 Geary Blvd., San Francisco (Richmond)
415.387.8273
10.30 – 22.00

All credit cards

Chinese medicine shop, Mountain View

HONGKONG-STYLE SEAFOOD

The Hongkong-style seafood house is Hongkong. It is the center of the social scene, where the ordinary and elite come to rub shoulders over steamed fish and shark's fin soup. It is a brash and sassy reflection of the city's attitude, replete with a deafening symphony of chatter, cheer, and chiming plates. Money talks here, much like how it does in the lofty chambers over Central: As long as you are willing to pay, you can eat any seafood exotica available to man. A trip to a seafood house therefore is destined to be a fascinating experience each and every time – not only for people watching but also for some of the best haute cuisine in Chinese cooking today.

Unlike the mom-and-pop operations of most Chinese restaurants, Hongkong-style seafood houses are usually built by capital investors. Run by a corporate style of governance, these restaurants have considerably more control in the quality and consistency of their menus. Innovation is the house rule, so don't expect much sentimentality to old traditions. Chefs routinely come up with strange new dishes, like scallops in XO sauce and abalone shabu shabu. Surprising new twists like shrimp with fried milk and lemon fish soup continue to keep customers coming back for more.

Incorporating both Guangdong and western elements in cooking, Hongkong-style seafood is much more refined than Guangdong cuisine. Often, simple cooking techniques of steaming and stir-frying are all that the seafood needs. Complex cooking procedures frequently throw off balance the delicate flavors of the sea. Or they are overwhelmed by too many ingredients. Hongkong-style seafood is none of that. In essence, it glorifies the simplicity of Guangdong cooking by embracing the natural flavors and textures of the ingredients. Hardly any other cooking style can be a better match for seafood.

LIVE FISH TANKS

You can immediately identify a Hongkong-style seafood house by the live fish tanks lining one side of the wall. Crabs, shrimp, clams, and saltwater fish are the standard offerings. In some upscale places the fish tanks are filled with exotic creatures for big appetites and bigger bank accounts. When they are in season, Maine lobsters are nearly obligatory. Favorite imported seafood items include geoduck clams (pronounced "gooey-duck") from the Pacific Northwest, halibut from Alaska, and imperial crabs from Australia.

Ordering seafood from the fish tanks is something unique and not found in other Chinese food experiences. Dishes with "seasonal price" next to them usually use the live seafood. These are frequently the chef's newest creations. You can also have the live seafood prepared to your specifications. Just tell the waiter exactly how you want the seafood cooked. They usually know all the possibilities, so they can be very helpful with suggestions.

COOKING METHODS FOR SEAFOOD:

Guangdong's cooking techniques are ideal for seafood, because they are simple and uncomplicated. This helps maintain their natural and delicate flavors. Basics such as steaming, boiling, stir-frying, and deep-frying are usually all that the seafood needs. More often than not, complex cooking methods, such as in Jiangzhe cuisine, actually do the seafood more harm than good.

Steaming
蒸

A perfectly steamed fish requires precise timing, based on the fish's weight and meat density. It is not as easy to do at home as it seems. The Chinese prefer fish steamed over any other way. A light reduction of soy sauce and fish stock is poured on top, garnished with a sprinkling of julienne ginger and scallions. Steamed fish usually comes with the head and tail intact. You can instruct to have the head removed, and served separately in an earthenware hotpot as a stew if you wish.

Steaming is also good for clams, oysters, and shrimp. These go well with a sauce of fermented black beans and chili, or with the similar garnish of julienne ginger and scallions.

Boiling
煮

Boiling is mostly used for shrimp and prawns. When they are in season, pinkish piles of boiled shrimp are seen on almost every table. Boiled shrimp are usually eaten as an appetizer. People peel the shrimp off their shells and dip them in a punchy soy sauce laced with fresh red chili. The Chinese never eat boiled lobsters, unlike Americans. Instead, the preferred cooking methods for lobster are steaming and "baking" (see below).

Stir-frying
炒

If a whole fish were to be eaten in two or more courses, the fillets can be stir-fried with fresh vegetables like asparagus, onions, or green peppers. Other stir-fried seafood favorites include kungpao shrimp and scallops stir-fried in XO sauce.

Deep-frying
泡

Often an entire fish is deep-fried with a light batter, and drizzled with a "red-cooked" or "Shanghai-style" sauce on top. Squid, scallops, and shrimp can also be deep-fried, served with a dish of salt and pepper for dipping. However, when it comes to skills, the Chinese are not the most consistent deep-fryers. No matter which Chinese restaurant, the food can be light and crispy one day, and greasy and soggy the next.

"Baking"
焗

A distinctive Guangdong cooking technique, "baking" is a technique in which ingredients are coated with starch or flour, deep-fried to a crisp, and then simmered in a soup stock. The starch in the fried pieces thickens the broth into a hearty stew, absorbing all the flavors of the ingredients. This technique is translated as baking, even though it shares no relationship to the oven-baking technique familiar in the West.

X MARKS THE XO SAUCE

Deeply immersed in the lore of Hongkong-style seafood is the XO sauce – a spicy condiment that has altered seafood dining for a generation. Pungent and spicy, the XO sauce is the perfect accompaniment to seafood. It has no equal in both popularity and influence within the league of Guangdong cooking sauces.

No one really knows exactly what goes into the XO sauce. Most agree the basics include dried scallops, dried shrimp, garlic, and chili peppers. The rest has piqued spirited speculation among foodies worldwide. One fact is absolutely certain: the XO sauce does not contain a single drop of XO, the French cognac that lends its name. "XO" is merely a marketing moniker used to command higher prices for the dishes that use them. A de facto status symbol, the "XO" name naturally carries a sophisticated weight with the image-conscious Chinese.

The inventor of the XO sauce is also unknown. Some speculate the credit belongs to Fook Lam Moon, a famous Kowloon seafood house. Faced with sagging sales in the mid-1960s, Fook Lam Moon sparked a sensation with this winning recipe. A firestorm swept through the entire Hongkong food scene as a result, and soon every other seafood house in town had to have their own XO sauce on the menu.

Today, the popularity of the XO sauce has not faded. A jar of it can be found in restaurants and home pantries alike. The pungency and spiciness are just right for most seafood. It is ideal for stir-frying squid, lobster, and scallops. Meats also get an instant makeover, like steamed spareribs and grilled steak.

Is the XO sauce the Alex Rodriguez of the Chinese pantry? Yes it is pricey. (A small jar costs around $15.) But it is worth every penny - capable of doing just about anything when called for in the kitchen. Perhaps this why the XO sauce is considered the best all-around condiment in the league of Chinese cooking sauces.

ACCOMPANYING SAUCES FOR SEAFOOD:

The basic sauces that accompany seafood have names like "Shanghai-style" and "Sichuan-style." They tell very little about what they are and how they taste like though. Moreover, each restaurant has its own way of doing things, so it is best to ask the waiter for a clarification.

"Red-Cooked" Sauce
紅燒

Often called "Shanghai-style," this sauce echoes the red-cooking method of Jiangzhe and Shanghai. In the manner typical of eastern China, a combination of black rice vinegar, soy sauce, and sugar is used to simmer fish. The reddish color gives this sweet and sour sauce its name. Sometimes ketchup is used for a fruitier sweet and sour dimension.

Sichuan-style
川式

The Sichuan style of preparing fish is to create a spicy sauce from minced chili peppers, garlic, and scallions. It is poured over steamed or deep-fried fish. In a Hongkong-style seafood house, the fieriness of Sichuan cooking is tamed considerably: the sauce will likely be sweet, slightly tart, and with just a hint of hotness in it.

Black Bean Sauce
豉椒

Made from fermented black beans or bean paste, this sauce has been a longtime favorite for steaming and stir-frying. Steamed pork spareribs, which shows up on nearly every dim sum cart, is the most popular application. The black bean sauce is used in steamed clams and half-shell oysters as well. Stir-fried crab, fish, and lobster also attain great heights with fragrances suggestive of raw soy sauce.

Sweet-and-sour (sugar-and-vinegar) Sauce
甜酸

Sweet-and-sour sauce, to a Chinese, is a brown sauce of black rice vinegar flecked with chopped scallions.

This sauce goes well with steamed fish and all kinds of deep-fried foods. To Americans, sweet-and-sour sauce is made with salted plums. Restaurants are capable of working with both kinds, but they usually assume Americans want the red plum sauce without asking.

XO Sauce

This is a popular condiment for meats and seafood (see separate section). On the menu, you will find many dishes using it, from stir-fried clams to even chow mein.

Salt-and-Pepper "Sauce"
椒鹽

Not really a sauce but a seasoning, this is a flavoring created by combining together salt, ground black pepper, and star anise. Salt-and-pepper always goes with deep-fried foods. It can either be coated onto the food by tossing, or served on the side as a dipping salt.

Garlic-and-chili "Sauce"
蒜爆

Also called "bursting garlic," this is another "sauce" that is more like the dipping salt-and-pepper seasoning above. Minced garlic is sautéed with hot green or red chili, and then tossed with deep-fried foods.

THE PROZAC AND VIAGRA OF CHINESE COOKERY

You can eat some of the most expensive Chinese meals at a seafood house. In particular, people woo over shark's fin and swallow's nest. Often these "seafood" items are so sought after that they fetch more than $100 per serving. And it is not unusual for the Chinese to drop $2,000 for a banquet table just to serve these things to families and friends.

But shark's fin is nothing more than cartilage, and swallow's nest is dried bird spittle. Both are also flavorless, so they do not add much of anything to the dish. However, the Chinese subscribe to the belief that all foods have some medicinal effects in them, and somehow shark's fin and swallow's nest are believed to possess powers to do wonders. Never substantiated by science, they are said to increase libido for men, and finer skin for women. The Chinese are so enchanted by them that that through many generations they are the Prozac and Viagra in Chinese cookery.

In Chinese medicine shops, you can buy different grades costing up to $1,000 a pound. Invariably, the sales clerk will suggest you need a six-month supply. This can translate into a month's worth of mortgage payments. Or you can come to a seafood house for an immediate gratification. Also invariably, the waiter will suggest the rarest (read: priciest) dishes for the most beneficial effects. Either way, you will be persuaded that shark's fin and swallow's nest are the panacea for everything, all except perhaps penury and your bottom line.

To meet the maddening demand for shark's fin and swallow's nest, the Chinese often go to the extremes in procuring them. The "harvesting" of swallow's nests requires men to scale rocky cliffs and caves. Obtaining shark's fins is especially known for its cruelty. Since the fins are much more valuable than the shark meat, fishermen waste no time in cutting off the fins at sea, then toss the helpless sharks overboard to drown. This practice of "finning" is banned in several western nations, including the U.S. and Australia. But they continue unabated throughout Asia with no regulatory oversight. Considering the endless flow of lucre from Chinese demand, finning will continue to be the main method of harvest. The rate of consumption is also threatening to deplete the world's shark population in the coming decades.

WHERE TO EAT SEAFOOD IN THE BAY AREA

Hongkong-style seafood houses are usually huge places, and usually located away from the city. They are not so big inside Chinatown because space is at a premium, but once outside, the proportions reach that of convention halls. Their brassy décor and rollicking atmosphere are almost required for absolute authenticity. Look for the live fish tanks by the door or along one side of the wall. A well-stocked tank is a good sign for a popular place. Don't hesitate to ask the waiter for advice about different ways to prepare the catch.

Fu Lam Moon Seafood Restaurant
富臨門海鮮酒家

1678 N. Milpitas Blvd., Milpitas
408.942.1888
17.00 – 00.00

All credit cards

Fook Yuen Seafood Restaurant
馥苑海鮮酒家

195 El Camino Real, Millbrae
650.692.8600
17.30 – 21.30

All credit cards

Koi Palace
鯉魚門海鮮茶寮

365 Gellert Blvd., Daly City
650.992.9000
17.00 - 21.30

All credit cards

Hong Kong Flower Lounge
香港香滿樓

51 Millbrae Ave., Millbrae
650.692.6666
17.00 – 21.30

All credit cards

Mayflower Restaurant
五月花酒家

428 Barber Ln., Milpitas
408.922.2700
17.00 – 21.30

All credit cards

6255 Geary Blvd., San Francisco (Richmond)
415.387.8338
17.00 – 21.30

All credit cards

ABC Seafood Restaurant
富豪皇宮海鮮酒家

768 Barber Ln., Milpitas
408.435.8888
17.00 - 21.30

All credit cards

Legendary Palace
燕喜樓

708 Franklin St., Oakland
510.663.9188
17.00 – 23.00

Mastercard, Visa

Saigon Seafood Harbor Restaurant
西貢漁港

3150 Pierce St., Richmond
510.559.9388
11.00 – 23.00

Mastercard, Visa

New Asia Chinese Restaurant
新亞洲大酒樓

772 Pacific Ave., Chinatown
415.391.6666
17.00 – 21.00

Mastercard, Visa

Great Eastern Restaurant
迠賓閣

649 Jackson St., Chinatown
415.986.2500
10.00 – 01.00

All credit cards

Harbor Village Restaurant
海景假日翠亨邨茶寮

4 Embarcadero Center, Lobby Level, San Francisco
415.781.7833
17.30 - 21.30

All credit cards

DIM SUM/YUM CHA

Contrary to popular belief, dim sum/yum cha was not invented in Hongkong. Rather, it evolved from a traditional breakfast eaten in Guangzhou, the nexus of southern Chinese cooking styles. People there eat a quick breakfast of two steamed dumplings with a pot of pu-er tea. This became popularly known as the "One Pot, Two Items" breakfast. Whereas the typical Chinese breakfast beverage is soymilk, in Guangzhou they drink tea. Thus, the inseparable association between dim sum and tea drinking is forever set in stone.

Chefs of the 1960s Hongkong food scene reformed the "One Pot, Two Items" tradition by converting the hearty dumplings into a sampling of smaller snacks. They also moved them out of small neighborhood restaurants and into the large seafood houses around town. Portions got smaller so that people could sample more varieties without filling quickly. Each piece is no more than a bite or two, and a typical meal usually involves three or four orders a person. Dim sum/yum cha is unique in Chinese food because it is not well-suited for large families or groups. Passing small baskets around a table of ten is rather awkward and burdensome, so this is a dining experience more appropriate for individuals or small groups of three or four.

Why does this book use the term *dim sum/yum cha*? Because both are interchangeable terms in Chinese. Dim sum means "snacks," and yum cha means "drinking tea." In actuality, the two terms used together best describe the whole experience, which is both the excitement of sampling snacks and the enjoyment of drinking tea. Incidentally, Australians have always called it "yum cha."

THE DINING MORES OF DIM SUM/YUM CHA

Unlike the rigid tea ceremony of Japan, the "yum cha" part of dim sum is relaxed and informal. However, tea drinking is obligatory, so once you are seated at the table, the waiter does not ask if you want tea, but what tea you want. The primary tea of choice is pu-er, the standard black tea of Guangdong. Common alternatives include jasmine, oolong, and ju-pu – a blend of pu-er with juhua (chrysanthemum flowers). It is said that pu-er and ju-pu have especially good grease-cutting abilities that are appropriate counterbalances for the richer, fattier contingent on the dim sum cart.

The dim sum/yum cha experience happens only for breakfast, but people routinely eat it well past lunchtime. Orders are taken by flagging down the women hawkers (men are never employed to hawk dim sum) who roam the dining room with a handcart or shoulder tray. The handcarts are actually a recent invention. The old way to order is a la carte: by checking off the items on a menu card placed on the table. Many of the trendiest dim sum/yum cha places today have returned to this way of service. Either way, just point to anything interesting to get your dim sum/yum cha action started.

DIM SUM SPOTTER'S GUIDE

There can be more than thirty dim sum dishes offered at one time, so the choices could be bewildering even for people familiar with the rite. Often orders are stacked four or five baskets high, or hidden under dome-covered plates. What is contained inside is not always obvious, but since the placement of the dishes is done in a more or less systematic manner, the appearance of the carts gives good indication of what they have inside. Other than that, the next best thing would be to guard your tableside like Checkpoint Charlie, and not let any hawker woman go by without a thorough interrogation. Here are some of the typical offerings:

SMALL STEAMER BASKETS

Har gow (shrimp jiaozi)
蝦餃
Small, bite-sized dumpling of whole shrimp and mashed shrimp, all wrapped in a translucent wrap made of rice flour. Har gow has a pale pink color from the shrimp inside.

SOUTHERN

Shao mai (pork dumpling)
燒賣

Pork filling is stuffed into an egg noodle wrap, and shaped to resemble a small teacup. It is yellow all around, except for the exposed top, where the steamed pork filling shows a slightly pinkish color.

Shark's Fin Jiaozi
魚翅餃

Shark fin adds extra mileage for this otherwise ordinary filling of pork. Don't count on extravagance though: expensive shark's fin is never used in a dumpling like this.

Fun gor
粉果

Typical Chinese dumplings are made with a flour wrap of some sort, but this Chaozhou specialty is made with a rice flour wrap. It is nearly transparent so that the contents inside are visible. Fillings for fun gor include shrimp, pork, and mint for a Southeast Asian tint.

Beef Meatballs
牛肉丸

These meatballs are lightly seasoned with soy sauce and steamed over a bed of spinach. Beef meatballs are not coated with any kind of sauce. They can be eaten either as they are, or dipped with chili sauce or mustard.

Fish Balls and Octopus Balls
魚蛋 ， 墨魚蛋

Fish balls are made of fish fillets pounded into a smooth paste, and octopus balls are a variation of fish balls with pieces of octopus mixed inside. Some places offer them with distinctively Chaozhou overtones: by steaming in curry and coconut milk.

Dumplings Wrapped in Tofu Skin
腐皮捲

Kind of like steamed egg rolls, tofu skin is used to wrap a vegetarian filling. Tofu and soybean byproducts are used extensively by Chinese vegetarians to create all sorts of meat-like textures. They also provide vital nutritional balance to the vegetarian diet.

LARGER STEAMER BASKETS

Nu Mi Gai (Glutinous Rice Chicken)
糯米雞

A meal in itself, a single portion is substantial enough for one's dim sum allotment. Of course, it can be shared with others so that there is room left for other dim sum. The hawker woman will cut open the lotus leaf-wrapped package, revealing a fragrant mound of glutinous rice inside, with a lightly seasoned piece of chicken stuffed in the center.

Red-cooked Chicken Feet
紅燒鳳爪

Chicken feet are steamed in a savory sauce slightly piqued with red chili. The feet should be steamed soft enough so that they melt in the mouth, capable of being eaten without hands. There is not much meat on the chicken feet, so what's the point? The Chinese love the gelatinous texture, which is why they pay big bucks for shark's fin, go crazy for boba, and make this dish an indispensable item on the dim sum cart.

Spareribs in Black-bean Sauce
豉汁排骨

A dish of pork spareribs is steamed in a black-bean sauce until the meat is tender. This is typical home cooking in Guangdong cuisine, normally served as a main entrée. Here, it is reduced to a bite-sized portion for the dim sum appetite.

Steamed Tripe
牛百葉

Cooked in a similar fashion as steamed spareribs, steamed tripe has a chewy texture that many people love. Fashionable dim sum restaurants make this dish in a spicy XO sauce.

Xiaolongbao (Soupy Dumplings)
小籠包

The smallish steamed baozi are filled with a meat filling and soup inside. It is not a Guangdong dish, but a Shanghai street snack (see page 146). Dim sum/yum cha houses mostly do a mediocre job with this dish since they are not specialists in that regard.

Assorted baozi
包子

There are all sorts of steamed baozi, including fillings of red beans (sweet), mashed lotus seeds with duck egg (combination of sweet and salty), and charsui (salty). Popular these days are green baozi, colored with spinach or another type of leafy greens.

PLATES SHIELDED BY DOME COVERS

Rice Chong Fun (rice noodle rolls)
蒸腸粉

Inside the dome covers contains a rice noodle roll called chong fun, which literally means "sausage-like rice noodles." They have an appearance resembling shiny white enchiladas. Chong fun are made by wrapping a broad, flat sheet of fun (rice noodle) with an assortment of fillings such as beef, shrimp, or charsui pork. Even the infamous youtiao can be wrapped. A light soy sauce is poured on top prior to serving. Chong fun can also be grilled, which is served from a cart with a roving grill (see below).

ASSORTMENT OF COLD CUTS

Shredded Jellyfish
海蜇皮

Preserved jellyfish is soaked in water to remove excess salt. Then it is cut into strips, marinated with salt and vinegar, and served like a cold salad. It looks like a mound of rubber bands, and tastes like it too. Otherwise flavorless, jellyfish has a slithery, crunchy texture, and absorbs all the flavors of the marinating sauce.

Cold Roast Duck
烤鴨

Leftover roast duck from the day before is served cold the morning after. It is coated with a thin sprinkling of au jus.

Cold Charsui Pork
叉燒肉

Just like cold roast duck, leftover charsui pork is chopped and served cold as a dim sum dish.

Boiled Chicken Feet
鹽水鳳爪

Unlike steamed chicken feet (see above), the boiled ones are eaten cold. They are also less well-done, so that they are not as tender and have a sinewy texture. Hands are required to eat these. The Chinese rarely dip these in chili, mustard, or soy sauce to enhance their light flavors.

Fried Taro Nuggets
炸芋角

Mashed taro is shaped into palm-sized nuggets, and stuffed with a filling made of ground pork. The golden, lacy outer layer of taro nuggets is created by deep-frying, which suggests that it is a warm item. However, these are actually cold dumplings.

SWEETS

White Sugar Cake
白糖糕

This soft rice cake is leavened and slightly fermented by yeast before steaming. It is cut into square pieces and served cold. A classic Guangdong tea pastry, it is eaten either for breakfast or throughout the day as an in-between-meals snack. The use of yeast shows European influences in Guangdong cooking. In fact, this is sometimes called "London Cake" for its perceived association with the English.

Coconut Milk Jelly
冰凍椰糕

The coconut used in this gelatin dessert gives the dish an unmistakably tropical and Southeast Asian character. Its presence on the dim sum cart shows the degree of refinery and sophistication that transformed Guangzhou's humble "One Pot, Two Items" breakfast into a meal with an international flair.

Egg Custard Tarts
蛋撻

Custards and tarts are learned from the French, and they are put together to create this gem. Egg custard tarts are so popular with the Chinese that they have become an obligatory member of the dim sum lineup. A creamy egg custard is baked into a flaky piecrust, showing masterful blending of western influences into Guangdong cuisine, using butter, cream, and eggs not typically used in Chinese cooking.

Some places serve a Macanese (from Macau) or "Portuguese" version that has a slight burnish of caramelized sugar on top the custard, something like a dim sum-style crème brûlée.

Sesame Paste Roll-ups
芝麻卷

Black sesame is grounded into a

paste, and rolled into bite-sized pieces. The flavor of toasted sesame matches well with tea, and the sweetness provides a good balance to other mainly salty dishes in dim sum/yum cha.

STEAMING POT OF BOILING WATER

Boiled Gai Lan
水煮芥蘭

This cart with a pot of boiling water serves a traditional dim sum/yum cha stalwart – blanched gai lan, often called "Chinese broccoli." Oyster sauce is poured on top upon serving.

ROVING GRILL

On the grill are usually three types of rice cakes: turnip rice cakes; water chestnut cakes; and chong fun – the rice noodle enchilada described above. Be patient with the hawker women. Grilling takes time, so this is always the slowest cart on the floor.

White Radish Cakes
蘿蔔糕

This steamed rice cake is flavored with white radish and flecks of Guangdong-style sausage. The rice cake is cut into square pieces, and grilled until brown on both sides.

Water Chestnut Cakes
馬蹄糕

This steamed rice cake has a yellow color, and is actually sweet. The unusual combination of flavors and textures makes the water chestnut cake a perennially popular item on the roving grill.

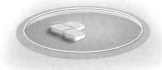

Chong fun
煎腸粉

Grilled chong fun can come with fillings of beef, pork, or shrimp. There are also plain rolls with no fillings at all. Instead of a topping of light soy sauce, as is the case with the steamed ones, grilled chong fun is served with one of two sauces: a sauce based on sweet bean paste; or a peanut sauce. Roasted white sesame is often sprinkled on top for some added texture.

LARGE RICE COOKERS OR POTS

Congee
皮蛋肉粥

Guangdong-style restaurants serve a large variety of congees, flavored with all sorts meat and vegetables. The standard congee variety is ground pork with thousand-year-old eggs. This is typically the only flavor of congee served in dim sum/yum cha.

Ox Stew with White Turnip
蘿蔔牛什湯

A fortifying bowl of ox stew contains table scraps: beef tripe, intestines, liver, and sometimes pig blood, simmered together with white radish in Chu Hou Sauce.

Douhua (Soymilk Gelatin)
豆花

Soymilk gelatin (pinyin: douhua) is eaten throughout China for breakfast. It is made from soymilk and edible plaster (see chapter on Dumplings & Noodles, page 105). Dim sum houses serve it very simply – hot and sweet, with sugar syrup poured on top. Sometimes it is called "tofu fa".

Zhongzi (see page 160)

WHERE TO HAVE DIM SUM/YUM CHA IN THE BAY AREA

There are so many places to go for dim sum around town, it's nearly impossible to account for them all. You can find the traditional "One Pot, Two Items" breakfasts at bakeries all over San Francisco's and Oakland's Chinatowns, but they hardly exist in the suburbs. For Hongkong-style dim sum, restaurants large and small have their own takes on the obligatory offerings of shao mai, har gow, and chong fun. Generally the differences between one and the other are minimal, but a few have evolved with some character of their own. These are the places where a dim sum visit is always an adventure.

Whether it is the old, the ordinary, or the new, dim sum is a treat that you will never grow tired of. But no one agrees on who has the best dim sum around town. In fact, it is a question more heatedly debated than trying to build a new runway at SFO. Here are some interesting dim sum places in the Bay Area.

Koi Palace
鯉魚門海鮮茶寮

Commensurate with the charming location, the dim sum here is quite elegant. You can get nearly every dim sum imaginable here, plus some more – from traditional har gow to xiaolongbao filled with Dungeness crabmeat. The interesting surprises, especially on weekends, approach some of the best in Vancouver. Koi Palace also serves a soothing turtle gelatin (guilinggao). Although this "snack" is generally available throughout the Bay Area, Koi Palace is one of a few places that actually does not deny you with an accurate English translation. Yes, it is made of turtle simmered with herbal medicine (most places call it "herbal jelly").

51 Millbrae Ave., Millbrae
650.692.6666
11.00 – 14.30, at 10.30 on weekends

All credit cards

Mayflower Restaurant
五月花酒家

The fancy seafood house dishes out some of the liveliest dim sum in the Bay Area. Stuffed scallops, fried quail, and shrimp roll-with-mango are stuff you won't find in too many other dim sum places. On weekends, come early or come prepared to wait and mingle with a decidedly affluent crowd.

428 Barber Ln., Milpitas
408.922.2700
11.00 – 14.30, at 10.00 on weekends

All credit cards

Legendary Palace
燕喜樓

The loud and crowded dining room sets an inviting scenario for good, wholesome dim sum. The action is fast paced, and often the line spills onto the streets. The dim sum selection doesn't stray from the norm, but it can stand up to anyone else's around the Bay.

708 Franklin St., Oakland
510.663.9188
10.00 – 14.30, at 09.00 on weekends

Mastercard, Visa

Yank Sing
羊城茶室

It's removed from Chinatown, and the selections are just as removed from what you would typically find in conventional dim sum places. The spinach dumpling looks like green tortellini, the tofu roll is wrapped in nori, and the shrimp roll looks like little goldfish. Everything else from shao mai to steamed pork ribs is done with a sophisticated touch. There is even Peking duck. This is some of the most expensive dim sum around, but expensive doesn't always mean it's the best in the class.

101 Spear St. (One Rincon Center)
415.957.9300
11.00 – 15.00 weekdays, 10.00 - 16.00 on weekends

All credit cards

49 Stevenson St., San Francisco (SOMA)
415.541.4949
11.00 – 15.00

All credit cards

Y. Ben House
會賓樓

At this busy dining hall, the roving carts dish out a fairly predictable lineup of dim sum dishes. Nothing is extraordinary or flamboyant, which is what you would expect from Chinatown anyway. But Y. Ben House does things consistently well, making the dim sum here among of the best in the neighborhood.

835 Pacific Ave., Chinatown
415.397.3168
07.00 – 15.00

Mastercard, Visa

Ton Kiang
東江

There are only about twenty dim sum dishes on the offering, but all are created with careful deliberation so every one is worth trying. You can see it in the different shapes and colors they come in. The ingredients are also a little different: shrimp-stuffed eggplant, pea sprout-filled dumplings, mushroom-and-shrimp fun gor, and so on. And the best thing: they are available all day every day, so you can enjoy them at your whim.

5821 Geary Blvd., San Francisco (Richmond)
415.387.8273
10.30 – 22.00

All credit cards

Traditional dim sum, San Francisco Chinatown

HONGKONG-STYLE COFFEESHOP

Americans have a way of stereotyping Chinese food with egg fu-yung, chop suey, and fortune cookies. But to the Chinese, these things are as foreign as uni, tamale, and *mille feuille*. Not to be outdone, the Chinese have their own view on "seafarer's food" (pinyin: yangcai). To them, the Americans that first arrived by sea (thus the term *seafarer*) and who (along with other Europeans) eventually dominated China for the next 100 or so years eat lots of Spam, macaroni, and oxtail soup. Is that a fair assessment of American food, or is it a bad case of culinary revenge?

In Hongkong, the Chinese fascination for American food manifests in an interesting breed of coffeeshops throughout the city. The dishes are quite strange to anyone unfamiliar with this type of cooking. In another way, these coffeeshops are a rational response to the sebaceous wasteland of McDonald's, KFC, and Pizza Hut. Hongkong-style coffeeshops are places where steaks, burgers, and pastas rub shoulders with curries, congees, and chow fun. A few of the dishes can pass for the same down-home grub that comforts a homesick expat, but mostly they are roughshod fusions of American and Chinese favorites, with no particular claim to a specific homeland.

Coffeeshops also have busy bars serving a full range of nonalcoholic drinks. There is more shaking going on there than at a Christina Aguilera concert. The slew of concoctions, just like the coffeeshop menu, can be quite the shock to the first-timer. While the timid can stay with cola, tea, or coffee, there is another world of Horlicks (a malted beverage like Ovaltine), jellies, and bobas. Further into the depths of coffeeshop beverageology lurks taro milkshakes, red bean shaved ice, and grass jelly. The coffeeshop, alas, is not just a place for coffee.

DISHES OF HONGKONG-STYLE COFFEESHOPS

The coffeeshop menu is very much like a Guangdong-style restaurant menu, in that the dishes are best described in categories. All kinds of ingredients are thrown together to create a bewildering combination of dishes, resulting in a menu that is as thick as the Holy Bible. Some small coffeeshops counter these comprehensive menus by offering just a limited selection of rice, pasta, and pizza.

Rice

The Chinese typically eat rice as their main staple, and they assume Americans do the same. However, they see Americans as pouring a sauce or soup on top. The most popular of the "American-style" are beef-and-tomato and a starchy sauce of minced-beef with scrambled eggs. Coffeeshops also serve many kinds of stir-fried dishes with geographic names. The "Singapore-style" is seasoned with curry. "Yangzhou-style" rice is pale without adding soy sauce. "Fuzhou-style" consists of a soup floating with pieces of roast duck, chicken, and shrimp. If you are still not sure where is what, ask the waiter.

Congee

Congee is leftover rice, boiled with water until it becomes a gooey slop. It is eaten for breakfast like cereal. In poorer parts of China, people eat congee with nothing more than a salty square of fermented tofu. In Guangdong, people dress up congee a few notches by throwing together different combinations of ingredients. Just about anything goes. The classic is pork with thousand-year-old eggs. Other head-spinning congees include seafood, meatballs, liver, liver-and-kidney, chicken, chicken-and-mushroom, and even tofu-with-corn.

Eggs

The Chinese do not generally eat eggs as eggs themselves. They use eggs as a side ingredient, but not as the primary element. Thus, they think of egg dishes as foreign, particularly American. Any kind of fried or scrambled eggs, from sunny-side-up to omelets, is served "American-style" with a pork chop, steak, or a chicken fillet on the side. In some coffeeshops you can even find Top Ramen served with a fried egg on top.

Spam

The Hongkong-style coffeeshop is perhaps the only place in the world where Spam is a prominent feature on the menu. The Hormel folks must be proud. In reality, Spam is wildly popular all over Asia, frequently used as a substitute for ham. Many people like it simply with plain rice. In coffeeshops, typical Spam dishes include Eggs and Spam, Spam macaroni, and Top Ramen with Spam.

Salads

Salads are a touch of exotica inside the Chinese dominion, because the Chinese rarely eat fresh, raw vegetables. It comes from an age-old misperception that raw vegetables cause illnesses, when the cause is more likely bad sanitation. In the coffeeshops, salads tend to undergo very little alteration: Caesar's salad, Cobb salad, and chicken salad all look like they could be served at a Denny's or Waffle House. Even the run-of-the-mill garden salad sticks closely to American standards.

Steaks and Pork Chops

It is rare to see thick slabs of steak or pork chop anywhere in Chinese cooking. For one, it is mighty difficult to eat them with chopsticks. Second, the economies of meat consumption are incongruent with poverty. Therefore, steaks represent the enviable American spirit: living excessively and to the fullest. Steaks are typically seasoned with just salt and pepper, and then grilled to order. Upon serving, a white wine sauce is doused on top. Sides of garden salad and plain rice are the typical companions.

Curries

Curry is popular in Hongkong, although the mild palates of Hongkongers generally maintain a no-fly zone for such firebrands as the madras or the vindaloo. Curries served in Hongkong-style coffeeshops tend to closely resemble Japanese: soupy, heavily starched, and overtly sweet. Beef, oxtail, and chicken curries are popular, as is a meatless curry poured on top of a breaded pork chop. These are typically served over plain or fried rice, but more adventurous souls can try them over spaghetti.

Spaghetti and Pastas

Coffeeshops serve spaghetti with an extraordinarily garlicky tomato sauce, just the way the Chinese like it. Curry, as is mentioned above, is also a popular choice over pasta. Other accompaniments include the likes of conch cooked in white-wine, oxtail soup, and seafood.

Chow Mein, Stir-fried Noodles, Instant Noodles

Chow mein is a clump of steamed egg noodles pan-fried to a crisp on the outside, and then with a sauce poured on top. Stir-fried noodles are more straightforward – all the ingredients are stir-fried in the wok. Some coffeeshops serve instant noodles, a curious but widespread practice all over Hongkong. It comes to you straight off the package, or perhaps with a fried egg or hot dog on top.

Oakland Chinatown

WHERE TO VISIT A COFFEESHOP IN THE BAY AREA

Hongkong-style coffeeshops are places to watch Chinese hipsters
in action. The crowd tilts to the young, with a healthy nerd quotient
balanced by black-clad hip-hoppers and the Princeton Review
demography. And the food plays an interesting sideshow. The
comprehensive menus are chock full of hybrid dishes from Hongkong,
Europe, and America. There are also Taiwanese *mutations* of the
Hongkong-style, with particular emphasis on fusing Japanese elements
into the dishes.

Sampling beverages is also a good reason to visit a coffeeshop. All
beverages are non-alcoholic, and icons such as Boba Tea and shaved
ice are just the beginning of the road to taro milkshakes and *yuanyang*
(half coffee and half black tea). It's an other-worldly experience into
the depths of Chinese beverageology worth at least a try.

Café Ophelia-Fremont
芳苑咖啡西餐

46801 Warm Springs Blvd., Fremont
510.668.0998
11.00 – 00.00

Mastercard, Visa

At this Taiwanese version of the
coffeeshop, Japanese influences
are particularly strong. Look for
bento boxes. Flavors like miso
and teriyaki are diffused here and
there. Western-inspired dishes
favor those popular in Taiwan
these days: tomato-based pastas,
German roasted pork knuckle,
and rack of lamb. Some of the
beverages here come floating with
boba or even konnyaku (pinyin:
jurue, or "yam cake" on the
menu).

Café Ophelia-Milpitas
芳苑岩燒西餐

Steaks are served on a slab of hot
stone, so they arrive sizzling on
the table. The idea is to allow the
meat and garnishes to cook a few
more minutes before eating. Both
Fremont (see above) and Milpitas
locations serve a popular soup
baked under a puff pastry dome.

Hotpots are also served, featuring several popular broths such as pickled Napa, numbing-hot, and Chinese herbal medicine.

516 Barber Ln., Milpitas
408.943.1020
11.30 – 22.00, until 00.00 on weekends

Mastercard, Visa

Cousin Café
表哥茶餐廳

The action here hovers around unusual combinations like eel-and-chicken baked rice, "beef brisket curry spaghetti" on a sizzling platter, and fried rice with salmon and pineapples. Steaks come doused with either a black pepper, garlic, teriyaki, or yellow onion sauce. If you find any of these dishes boring, Top Ramen with Spam is also on the menu.

39193 Cedar Blvd., Newark
510.713.9806
08.00 – 23.00, until 01.00 on weekends

Cash only

Café 97
97 港式西餐

Small eateries like this are typical throughout Hongkong neighborhoods. They basically twist out hybrid versions of classic Guangdong rice and noodles. Shrimp fried rice is enhanced with pineapples, and Spam macaroni can be served with a fried egg on the side, if you like. If all this fusion stuff is too much to take, perhaps a grilled pork chop with fries will ease things.

1701 Lundy Ave., #160, San Jose
408.573.8208
11.00 – 22.00

Cash only

D&A Café
文記茶餐廳

Don't overlook the grittiness of this place. Good, soulful fare is served day and night at this Chinatown corner spot. You can choose from instant noodles to macaroni; chow fun to curry. Also try the "House Boil Chicken," which is their version of Hainan Chicken Rice.

702 Webster St., Oakland
510.839.6223
08.00 – 19.00

Cash only

Orchid Bowl Café
澳門街

Quite a rarity anywhere in North America is Macanese (from Macau) cooking. This place serves up a full menu of it. Although they are similar with the Hongkong prototype, the European-inspired dishes have more Portuguese influences. Chicken feet in abalone sauce, clam and taro congee, and baked spaghetti with pork chop are just some of the starters to a wholly different eating adventure.

3288 Pierce St., #C156, Richmond
510.559.7888
11.00 – 22.00

Mastercard, Visa

Sterling Ruby Restaurant
紅寶石餐廳

The filet mignon with black pepper sauce looks decidedly western. The chicken teriyaki is quite Japanese. The Hainan chicken rice is Chinese with Southeast Asia written all over it, and the ox tail curry has, well, no particular allegiance to anywhere. This is the gist of the coffeeshop experience, which for Chinatown is a dramatic turnaround from the lean pickings of nonstop Guangdong.

640 Jackson St., Chinatown
415.982.0618
07.30 – 21.30

Mastercard, Visa

Washington Bakery & Restaurant
華盛頓茶餐廳

This large and airy coffeeshop receives a constant stream of customers, who come here for a full menu of east-meets-west favorites. This is where you can get duck-and-oyster congee, beef tongue-and-tomato baked rice, and seafood curry. Finish off with milk with cream soda, honeydew tapioca, or a refreshing papaya-and-orange juice.

733 Washington St., Chinatown
415.397.3232
07.30 – 21.00

Mastercard, Visa

CHAOZHOU CUISINE

When the Americans left Saigon in 1975, the outcome of the Vietnam War was obvious to everyone. For the ethnic Chinese living in South Vietnam at the time, this was the beginning of a tumultuous odyssey that plunged them into years of unbelievable suffering. Most eventually fled the country. Many went back to their Guangdong homelands. Others drifted off in boats. The odyssey of the latter became well known throughout the world as the story of the Vietnamese Boat People.

Up to half of the Boat People perished at sea, but those who made it to America have graced us with their unique way of cooking, which takes Chinese cooking foundations to a level with Southeast Asian overtones. Thai and Vietnamese influences are particularly strong. The biggest distinctions include the use of fresh herbs like mint, lemongrass, and basil. Fish sauce, another common ingredient in Thai and Vietnamese cooking, also plays an integral part of Chaozhou cuisine.

Chaozhou cooking is also laden with chili peppers. Included in the Chaozhou pantry are many different types of chili pastes and hot sauces. The most important is the sriracha chili sauce, frequently referred as "Thai ketchup." In fact, a Chinese restaurant that has bottles of sriracha chili sauce on the tables is an instant giveaway as a Chaozhou-style restaurant.

Seafood is a notable specialty, prepared in similar ways as Hongkong-style seafood, but with much lighter characters. Southeast Asian flavors are always present, with herbs like mint and lemongrass making frequent overtures. Dishes are hot but not spicy, and because many herbs are used, the flavors can be quite complex. With exception of curry, Chaozhou cooking uses very little spice. It is worth comparing the flavors of Chaozhou-style seafood with that of Hongkong, both of which are exemplary styles of preparing crabs, fish, and lobsters.

TYPICAL CHAOZHOU-STYLE DISHES

Master-cooked Duck
潮州滷水鴨

Cooked in a brine of soy sauce and star anise, master-cooked ducks are a Chaozhou specialty. They have a rich, savory flavor more complex than the simple looks would suggest. Chopped into pieces, the duck can be served with hu tieu or rice. As an appetizer or main course, the duck can be served with tofu that is master-cooked in the same brine. The master-cooking method can be applied to beef and chicken as well.

Steak Salad (Beef Loc Lac)
法式牛柳

An interesting Cambodian dish, it is sometimes called "French-style Beefsteak." This salad features pieces of cubed grilled beefsteak, marinated in a tangy sauce of lime or tamarind water, and punctuated by the mildly sweet, cool sensations of seared mint leaves. The steak is served with whole lettuce leaves, and can be either eaten like a salad or wrapped taco-style.

Hot-and-sour Shrimp Soup, Thai-style
泰式蝦湯

A soup that is very similar to Thailand's Tom Yum Koong, this hot-and-sour soup gets its flavors from lemongrass, lime leaves, fish sauce, and lots of chili peppers. Although it is very spicy, the overall dimensions of the soup remain light and refreshing. It is ideally suited for eating during the summer.

Hot-and-sour Fish Soup, Vietnamese-style
越式魚湯

The Vietnamese version of the hot-and-sour soup, or canh chua, calls for a tangy, light fish broth flavored with pineapples, star fruit, tamarind, bean sprouts, and chili peppers. Like the Thai-version, it is preferably eaten very hot and spicy, and ideal for the summer months.

Thai Curry Crab
泰式咖哩焗蟹

A very popular Chaozhou dish, the curry sauce used over the fried crab is quite spicy, although it is much sweeter than the curry commonly associated with Indian cuisine. Some Chaozhou-style restaurants use coconut milk for a richer, more tropical flavor; others stick with ordinary stock and fish sauce.

Scallop and Asparagus with Mint
香葉蘆筍帶子

When scallops, asparagus, and mint are stir-fried together, the delicate flavors of the three ingredients come alive. However, none of the flavors overpowers the other, and the dish remains light, with subtle hints of the sea and the earth playfully intermixing within the dish.

Crab in Tamarind Sauce
酸枳螃蟹

Tamarind is used throughout Southeast Asia, but it is nearly unheard of elsewhere in Chinese cuisine. The sour, tangy flavors of tamarind are used for both cooking and confectionery. At the same time, they add a distinctly tropical dimension to the dishes. Crab in Tamarind Sauce is a simple dish featuring fried crab drizzled with a lightly seasoned sour sauce derived from tamarind water.

Boiled Prawns
新鮮大蝦

Boiled prawns are served with fresh slices of honeydew melon and cantaloupe, along with a dipping sauce made from oranges. The tartness of the orange sauce complements well the lightness of the boiled shrimp and sweetness of the fruits.

Frog Legs with Lemon Grass
香茅田雞

Saying that frog legs taste like chicken is not a cliché. Loosely translated, the Chaozhou people euphemistically call them "field chickens." A stir-fry of frog legs with a light sauce flavored with lemongrass and sriracha chili sauce reveals unmistakably Southeast Asian characteristics – light yet refreshingly hot.

HAINAN CHICKEN RICE

Hainan is a tropical island at the southernmost tip of China. Once part of Guangdong province, it is now a separate province to itself. In the 1850s, Hainan was on the direct route of the Chaozhou people's migration to Southeast Asia. Many migrants stopped there for provisions and supplies before continuing, and some local Hainanese joined in as well. In the process, a simple local dish of boiled chickens found new roosting grounds in the places where they settled: Malaysia, Thailand, Vietnam, and Singapore. This dish eventually evolved into the Hainan Chicken Rice, which is so popular in Singapore today that it is its *de facto* national dish.

Hainan Chicken Rice is comprised of a boiled chicken quarter, chopped and then served over a pile of plain rice. According to purists, the chicken must be a large hen, which renders large amounts of fat when cooked. The chicken is boiled until it is very tender. This is very different from the Guangdong-style of boiled chickens found in the barbecue shops (see page 19). Boiled chickens in the Guangdong style are left slightly underdone, with red blood still visible in the bones. This maintains a chewy, *al dente* texture in the meat, which they prefer. By contrast, Hainan-style boiled chickens are well-cooked and tender, so that the meat easily falls off the bones.

Long-grained Thai or jasmine rice is typically used. It further adds an unmistakable Southeast Asian touch. The rice is drizzled with chicken fat just prior to serving, so that it soaks up all of the chicken's essential flavors. Fried chicken is a recent diversion, but just like Hainan Chicken Rice, the fat-drizzled-rice remains essential to the main character of the dish.

Also sticking with tradition, there should always be three dipping sauces accompanying the Hainan Chicken Rice: a sweet soy sauce, a sauce of minced ginger marinated in oil, and a spicy *sambal* of fresh red chili and lime juice (the Malaysian equivalent of *salsa*). Places that do not serve up the trio instantly expose themselves as non-contenders to the Hainan Chicken trade.

Hainan Chicken Rice can be found in the usual culprits of Southeast Asian cuisines, including Malaysian, Thai, Vietnamese, and Chaozhou-style restaurants. It is also a regular staple in Hongkong-style coffeeshops. As is the customary practice, Hainan Chicken Rice is eaten with a fork and spoon, and *never* with chopsticks.

FAMILY HU TIEU

Chaozhou-style noodle chains are now an institution in the South Bay. In nearly every strip mall you will find either a TK Noodle or a New Tung Kee. Their menus are nearly identical, and everything down to the florescent lights is similar. Coincidence? Copycat? There's a story behind it.

This is the hu tieu version of the Mondavi rivalry. You know: brothers Peter and Robert have a fight and the world ends up blessedly with two great wineries. The Lu family had a similar fall-out, and now the Bay Area has two great noodle chains jostling for your appetite.

Mr. Lu Tan and his wife Du Ahn opened up the first Tung Kee Noodle Shop in San Jose in 1983. The Chaozhou family had escaped from Vietnam in 1978, at the beginning of the Boat People refugee wave. Together they made it to California, and worked tirelessly to make their business work. Eventually they built their little noodle shop into a chain of fifteen "TK Noodle"s from San Jose to Sacramento. It is a feat rarely accomplished by immigrant mom-and-pops.

Family disagreements led to the split between Lu and his relative business partners. This spawned the "New Tung Kee," which now has six highly visible locations. So far, both sides are keeping a peaceful but cold coexistence. Each noodle chain has maintained a distance from the other; as yet there are no two dueling things out at the same location. So, as long as business remains good, perhaps a little family rivalry like this isn't bad.

TK Noodle
Hu tieus, chow meins, "flour cakes."

15 locations.

www.tknoodle.com

New Tung Kee Noodle House
Hu tieus, chow meins, fried-rice, pad thais, "flour cakes."

6 locations.

www.newtungkeenoodle.com

RICE NOODLE DISHES

Rice noodles are eaten more frequently in Southeast Asia than any area of China. Their uses are very much like flour-based noodles. They are never deep-fried, however, because rice noodles contain more water content. Many of the Chaozhou-style rice noodle dishes resemble chow fun served in Guangdong-style eateries.

Hu tieu
粿條

The most important – and instantly recognizable Chaozhou-style rice noodle is the versatile hu tieu. It resembles Vietnamese pho, and in most cases they are interchangeable with little detectable difference. Ingredients that are used in hu tieu dishes can be any combination of meats, seafood, and vegetables – just like the rest of Guangdong cooking. Typical dishes include Chaozhou-style Duck Hu Tieu, Rice and Egg Hu Tieu, and Stir-fried Satay Beef Hu Tieu.

Bahn Loc
粘米粉

This is a different type of rice noodle. Bahn loc is made from a particular type of rice that has a high starch content. The rice flour dough is pressed through a sieve, creating short, slippery slivers that are thick in the middle and tapered at the ends. The coarse, uneven texture of the bahn loc is its main attraction. It has similar appeal as the knife-cut noodles of northern China.

Fish Balls
魚蛋

A method of preserving fresh fish is by pounding fish fillets into a paste, and then shaping it into marble-sized balls. Once cooked, fish balls have a firm, chewy texture, and can be used in place of meats in stir-fries, soups, and noodle dishes. Fish balls are also one of the few truly healthy foods in all of Chinese cuisine. They are low in cholesterol and fat, as well as having high nutritional values inherent in fish.

WHERE TO EAT CHAOZHOU IN THE BAY AREA

Chaozhou and Guangdong cookings share a common lineage, but have developed into very different cuisines. Most Chaozhou-style restaurants in town are small shops serving rice and rice noodles (hu tieu). Nearly all have a shop window stocked with master-cooked ducks. Don't mistake those with a Guangdong-style barbecue. The absence of charsui pork and suckling pig is the usual giveaway. Look for bottles of Siracha chili sauce on every table. It is the absolutely obligatory enhancement to any rice or noodle dish.

There is another type of Chaozhou-style restaurant serving seafood. Though more plebian in scale and substance when compared with Hongkong-style seafood, Chaozhou seafood is currently the rage on the west coast, and is giving the Hongkong prototype a run for the money. Dishes are considerably lighter, yet are surprisingly more complex with a larger combination of ingredients.

Kim Tar Restaurant
金塔粿條燒臘飯店

1698 Hostetter Rd., #J, San Jose
408.453.2006
10.30 – 00.00, at 09.30 on weekends

Cash only

Kim Tar makes its own hu tieu, which they sell to Asian markets nationwide. An archetypal Chaozhou-style restaurant, the place serves a collection of Chinese and Southeast Asian dishes. Un-Chinese flavors include curry, mint, and tamarind. The Vietnamese hot-and-sour shrimp soup (cahn chua tom) is very popular. Other homey seafood dishes feature frogs, clams, oysters, and scallops.

Golden Island Chinese Cuisine
金島潮州酒家

A one of a kind in the Bay Area, really. This places serves Chaozhou-style seafood as it exists on the mainland – without Southeast Asian influences. The dishes area considerably lighter than the Hongkong style, yet the flavors are more complex through a creative mix of ingredients.

Well-known specialties include stuffed sea cucumbers, braised fish bladder, and oyster omelet.

282-286 Barber Ct., Milpitas
408.383.9898
17.00 – 22.00

All credit cards

Vien Huong Restaurant
遠香蔴室

This simple rice and noodle shop serves comfort food offered in ample proportions. Some of the hu tieu ("ho fun" on the menu) and bahn loc dishes echo flavors of Cambodia and Vietnam. You can also have them with fish balls or beef satay. Others dishes are straightforward Chinese, like beef with broccoli. The crowd at lunchtime may require a wait.

712 Franklin St., Oakland
510.465.5938
07.30 – 19.00

Cash only

Capitol Kim Tar Restaurant
金塔粿條麵

The style here is more Chinese than Vietnamese, but things like beef satay and Thai curry chicken show some Southeast Asian influences. The house-made fish balls are a Capital Kim Tar specialty. They can be served in a noodle soup, or by themselves in curry. Another thing worth trying is the "house special salty duck," which is the Chaozhou-style master-cooked duck.

758 Pacific Ave., Chinatown
415.956.8533
09.00 – 21.00

Cash only

HUNAN CUISINE

Hunan cuisine remains the one of the most traditional forms of regional Chinese cooking. It adheres to a rural character: hearty, generous, and practical. Located between Guangdong and Sichuan provinces, Hunan cuisine is also an interesting blend of Guangdong and Sichuan cooking styles. This is an interesting combination because Guangdong and Sichuan cuisines are often at polar opposites in terms of flavor and style. Guangdong cuisine is light and prefers the natural flavors of the ingredients. Sichuan cuisine on the other hand is hot and spicy, and uses many ingredients to construct complex flavors.

Like Guangdong cuisine, Hunan dishes feature many fresh and local ingredients. However, flavors are much heavier, with liberal use of spices and condiments. Like Sichuan, Hunan dishes use a lot of hot chili peppers. However, Hunan treats chili peppers like a *vegetable*, often eating them fresh. This is rarely seen in Sichuan cuisine.

New York led America through a period in the 1970s when "Hunan" and "Szechwan" restaurants were the vogue of Chinatown. For the first time, Chinese food was given a spicy makeover with dishes like General Tso's Chicken and "Szechwan Beef." However, these were not really traditional Hunan or Sichuan cooking, but stylized takeouts with a few extra slivers of chili thrown in. This left main streets with a slew of "Hunan" restaurants that unfortunately speak very little of the actual Hunan style. While a few Hunan specialties, such as larou, can be found here and there, authentic Hunan cuisine is actually very difficult to find.

TYPICAL HUNAN-STYLE DISHES

Hunan cuisine is also called Xiang (Shiang) cuisine. The Chinese describe the style of cooking as "la and la." It is both hot (pinyin: la) like Sichuan cooking, and uses waxified meats ("la"-rou) extensively. Hunan cuisine can also be considered as a hybrid of Guangdong and Sichuan cuisines. The extent of their influences varies dish by dish, however.

Larou (waxified meats)
臘肉

The most famous element in Hunan cuisine is its method of preserving meats, with pork being the most important. Salted and cured, the meat hardens to resemble a reddish block of wax. The Hunan people call this meat larou, meaning "waxified meat." Some people just translate it as "Chinese ham." Larou can be used in a variety of dishes, from stir-fries to soups. It contains enough salt so that any dish that uses it does not need any further seasonings.

Pigeon Soup Steamed in Bamboo Cups
竹節鴿盅

This is one of the most unique and famous of Hunan dishes. Minced pigeon is steamed in its broth inside a bamboo cup (which is not edible). The gamy taste of the pigeon is balanced by the delicate and sweet flavors of the bamboo. Each cup makes an individual serving; the portion is small so it is often served as an appetizer. This popular dish also frequently shows up in banquets.

Minced Squab Wrapped in Lettuce Leaf
炒明蝦鬆

Minced squab is sautéed, then wrapped with lettuce leaves at the table to be eaten like a taco. It is a good appetizer dish, and is frequently served in banquets. Some restaurants also offer chicken and shrimp as alternatives to the sautéed squab.

General Tso's Chicken
左宗棠雞

There was indeed a General Tso. He was a Qing Dynasty official from Hunan who went to Beijing to serve the emperor. However, he longed for his home cooking so much that he took it on himself to cook this favorite dish every day. Diced chicken is deep-fried until crispy, and then coated with a fiery sauce of red chili peppers, garlic, soy sauce and vinegar. In America, this recipe is altered by using plum sauce, orange juice, and even pineapples. However, the basic elements: deep-fried chicken, tangy sauce, and spicy flavors continue to be General Tso's Chicken's distinguishing characteristics.

Steamed Chicken, Hunan-style
富貴雞

This is one of the most famous Hunan dishes. A whole chicken is marinated with spices and steamed in a lotus leaf wrap. In some restaurants, the steamed chicken is also stuffed with glutinous rice and ham. The flavors absorbed from the lotus leaf are what give the dish its unique characteristics.

Larou Stir-fried with Leeks
蒜苗臘肉

Generally, larou can be stir-fried with any vegetable for a quick and down-home dish. The saltiness of larou goes very well with the freshness of any green vegetables. Chili peppers enliven the dish with an added dash of spiciness. Other common vegetables in this stir-fry include fresh garlic sprouts and dried white radish.

Baked Larou in Honey Sauce
富貴火腿

You can call it honey-baked ham if you want. Slices of baked larou are coated with a golden, cloying honey sauce, and served between two slices of plain white toast. It is eaten like a finger sandwich, usually as an appetizer. It is also served occasionally at banquets

Tofu Sheet Crisps
酥烤素方

Tofu sheets are stacked and pressed together to form a thin wafer, then fried until crispy. They are cut into strips, like flat tortilla chips, and served in a hand sandwich just like the larou described above.

Crispy Clarion Bells
酥炸響鈴

The fancy name obfuscates the mundane truth about this dish: fried wontons. The redeeming difference is that these "bells" are wrapped in thin tofu skins instead of flour sheets. The meat filling is pork, just like other wontons. The crunchy sound when biting into these resembles jingling bells, giving the dish its clever name.

Steamed Fish with Fried Bean Sauce
豆酥鱈魚

A fish fillet is plainly steamed at first, and then covered with a "sauce" made from deep-fried fermented soybeans. The beans actually come out like a garnish, which adds an extra crunchy dimension to the tenderness of the fish.

Stir-fried Beef and Red Chili Peppers
辣炒牛肉

Nothing can be simpler than this country dish, yet it illustrates the essence of Hunan. Shredded beef and red chili peppers are stir-fried together with soy sauce. It is hot like Sichuan, and the use of fresh chilis echoes Guangdong's preference for fresh and natural flavors.

WHERE TO EAT HUNAN IN THE BAY AREA

There are Hunan restaurants, and there are "Hunan" restaurants.
The latter came from the "Hunan and Szechwan" wave of Chinese
restaurants that started in New York in the 1970s. They had little to
do with real Hunan cooking; rather, they were glorified Guangdong
takeouts with extra chili peppers. But they did introduce America to
some of Hunan's specialties, like larou (sometimes called Chinese
ham), minced squab in lettuce leaf, and General Tso's Chicken.
Howecer, the rest of Hunan's rustic flavors remain largely at home.

Authentic Hunan cuisine therefore remains an obscurity stateside, due
in part because there are only a few Hunan natives here. Even with the
recent influx of mainland immigrants, the situation has not changed.
Also, because Hunan cuisine acts like a fusion of Guangdong and
Sichuan, it is routinely left in the shadows of those two. It's not all
hopeless though; the two "Hunan" restaurants below have enough of a
regional character to give graspable glimpses into this style of cooking.

Chili Garden Restaurant
火宮殿

If you stick with the English
menu, this is another nondescript
strip mall takeout. Inconveniently,
all of the spectacular dishes are
on the Chinese-only menu. They
include a downright-homey stir-
fry of ground pork and diced
pickled string beans – a favorite of
Mao Zedong during his dictatorial
life. Larou is stir-fried with garlic
sprouts, leeks, or preserved white
radishes. It can also be simmered
with konnyaku, a house specialty.
Badger the staff for translations,
and convince them to print the
stuff out in English one day.

3213 Walnut Ave., Fremont
510.792.8945
11.30 – 21.30

Mastercard, Visa

Brandy Ho's Hunan Food
何家湖南

The creativeness of the dishes you find here means that Brandy Ho's has irreversibly strayed from the "old country." But that's quite okay. Considering the "calamari with curry and wine sauce," hot-and-sour beef," and "shredded pork with celery," Hunan cuisine has potential to go far and wide in this cosmopolitan town. The "smoked products" are the house version of traditional larou (waxified meats). They have pork, chicken, and duck available every day.

217 Columbus Ave., Chinatown
415.788.7527
11.00 – 23.30

All credit cards

HAKKA CUISINE

The full story of the Hakkas is a mystery even to most Chinese. No one can fully exact an account of their history, nor explain why they are considered an ethnic minority. After all, there are no traceable roots distinguishing the Hakkas from the Hans. However, because they do not have a historical homeland, the Hakkas are the literal "Guest People" of China, forced to migrate repeatedly over the past millennium.

Hakka cuisine reflects the frugal lifestyle of these constant migrants. No seafood is spoken for in the cuisine. Fresh vegetables are also rare, replaced by a wide assortment of preserved and fermented foodstuffs. These are also the primary condiments in their cooking, because they contain plenty of salt for all the necessary flavorings. Fermented mustard greens, salted white radishes, and fermented tofu are typical examples. From them, Hakka dishes have the reputation for being disarmingly salty, and with very heavy flavors.

Pork and poultry are the primary meats consumed. Always being frugal, all parts of the animal are eaten. Dishes with pig intestines are very popular. A favorite way of preparation is to deep-fry an entire length of it stuffed with scallions. The intestines are then chopped and served with julienne ginger and yellow rice vinegar as dip. Another typical Hakka dish is tripe stir-fried with pineapples. Other table scraps are boiled in plain water, and served simply with a dipping sauce of soy sauce mixed with fermented orange paste.

Among the repertory of cooking techniques, steaming is the most important. Probably the most famous Hakka dish is *kourou*: pork belly slices steamed in a bowl with chopped fermented mustard greens. You can also find kourou in Jiangzhe cuisine (see page 139), which suggests the Hakkas picked up this dish as they passed through the region centuries ago on their migration southward.

THE FEW STANDOUT HAKKA DISHES

Four famous dishes, described below, stand out in Hakka cuisine. The Chinese seldom mention the rest of Hakka cuisine, which is a crude collection of offal and fermented foodstuffs. The Hakka kitchen resembles a cross of the high school biology lab with the home economics class: Lots of innards and rudimentary cooking, which explain the cuisine's relative obscurity.

Kourou with Fermented Mustard Greens
梅乾菜扣肉

The dish of steamed slices of pork belly (kourou) is immediately identifiable as Hakka, even though its roots probably stem to the Jiangzhe region in eastern China. Fermented mustard greens, seasoned with soy sauce and star anise, is steamed with pork belly slices in a large bowl. This dish displays all three major characteristics of Hakka cooking: using pork is the primary meat in the diet; relying on fermented foodstuffs for flavor; and steaming, which plays a larger role in Hakka cooking than in any other region.

Niang (stuffed) Tofu
釀豆腐

The technique of stuffing meats into vegetables (pinyin: niang) is now considered a classic in Hakka cuisine. The history of the technique reaches as far back as 300 years, from the Ming Dynasty. The original dish called for pork stuffed in a cube of tofu, but almost any vegetable could be stuffed in lieu of tofu. Popular variations include fish paste stuffed in bell peppers and shrimp stuffed in bittermelon.

Three-cups Chicken
三杯雞

This dish originated from a Hakka district in Jiangxi province where, according to legend, a housewife stewed a chicken for the ancestral prayer with the only ingredients available in the pantry: a cup of oil, a cup of rice wine, and a cup of soy sauce. Fresh basil provided additional flavors. As the use of basil is quite unusual in the rest of Chinese cooking, this has become the distinguishing characteristic for this dish. Typically, this dish is served in the same earthenware hotpot in which it is cooked. Also, with increased health consciousness, the cup of oil is replaced by a cup of water.

Dongjiang-style Salt Roasted Chicken
東江鹽焗雞

Along the Dongjiang (East River), near Guangzhou, is a stretch of Hakka communities. Thus the "Dongjiang" descriptor before the dish usually suggests Hakka roots. The local specialty is a whole chicken wrapped in paper and roasted in a mound of salt. This is a time-consuming process, and most restaurants cut corners by boiling the chicken first, or roasting it in an oven without any salt. You can find salt roasted chicken in nearly all Guangdong-style restaurants. If you ever wondered what those chickens wrapped in wax paper hanging in the barbecue shelves are, these are it.

Salt roasted chicken

Rose apples

WHERE TO EAT HAKKA IN THE BAY AREA

To say that the Hakkas can't cook may be an understatement; the few "Hakka" restaurants around town actually have more Guangdong dishes. Therefore, an authentic Hakka experience is nearly impossible to find. Instead, the four famous Hakka dishes can be found here and there on the menus of all regional types. You can always find the salt-roasted chicken, niang (stuffed) tofu, and kourou with fermented mustard greens. Three-cups chicken is more popular in Taiwanese restaurants.

Confusingly, because Hakka dishes are largely unknown to Americans, there are no consistent English names for them. There are more ways to translate "steamed pork belly in fermented mustard greens" than flavors at Baskin Robins. Even the Chinese name (pinyin: meigancai kourou) is a mouthful. Otherwise, look for the "Dongjiang" (East River) descriptor on the menu. It's a giveaway for a Hakka-influenced dish. Variant spellings include "Tung Kong" and "Ton Koon."

Hakka Restaurant
客人之家

Contrary to the name, there is nary a hint of Hakka at this busy joint. And the restaurant makes no pretense about it. If you ask they'll tell you this isn't really a Hakka restaurant. The only two Hakka dishes are: "stuffed bean cake," which is the Hakka classic niang tofu; and the "rock salted chicken," which is a distant approximation of the traditional salt-roasting recipe. But this place does brisk business every day – perhaps exactly because it has strayed so far from its Hakka roots.

137 E. 3rd Ave., San Mateo
650.348.3559
11.00 – 21.00

Mastercard, Visa

Ton Kiang
東江

Three of the four Hakka classics are tucked inside a menu, which is otherwise filled with interesting Guangdong dishes. Look for the "steamed salt baked chicken," "steamed bacon with dried mustard greens," and stuffed eggplant (and also tofu). The place also has impressive dim sum, served all day.

5821 Geary Blvd., San Francisco (Richmond)
415.387.8273
10.30 – 22.00

All credit cards

Dragon River Restaurant
龍江飯店

The "Hakka special dishes" on the menu include stuffed tofu. They can be steamed, deep-fried, or braised in fermented rice wine mash. Kourou comes steamed with fermented mustard greens – the traditional recipe, or with taro slices. There are also a couple of pork intestine dishes (deep-fried sections or braised in wine mash), but that is as far Hakka as it will go here.

5045 Geary Blvd., San Francisco (Richmond)
415.387.8512
11.00 – 21.30

Mastercard, Visa

Mon Kiang Restaurant
梅江飯店

You can actually attempt a decent Hakka meal here. The stuffed tofu, kourou, and salt-roasted chicken are found under the "Hakka's special dishes". Combine them with stir-fried tripe and deep-fried pork intestines for a rustic sojourn into faded history. To add a perky twist, try the beef or chicken with ginger and pineapples.

683 Broadway St., Chinatown
415.421.2015
11.00 – 22.00

Mastercard, Visa

FUJIAN CUISINE

It does not take much to dismiss Fujian cuisine, and many Chinese do just that – they routinely ignore it. Having to share the spotlight with heavyweight divas as neighbors: Guangdong to the south and Jiangzhe to the north; Fujian cuisine is the Not Ready For Prime Time Player on the pan-China stage.

Two things define Fujian cuisine: soups and the red fermented rice mash. For soups, many Fujian dishes are boiled or braised in one sort of soup stock or another. There is a local saying, "Give me some soup stock, and I'll show you ten dishes." The prevalence of boiling and braising in Fujian cooking contradicts the common perception that Chinese food is mostly stir-fried.

The red fermented rice mash is made from glutinous rice and red brewer's yeast. Wine produced in the fermentation process gives dishes an unmistakably earthy flavor. The mash can be applied to all varieties of meats, from pork to seafood. Because its penetrating flavors are best enhanced through slow cooking, the wine mash is usually used in soups and sauces. This further substantiates the large number of soupy dishes in Fujian cooking.

Overall, the entire curriculum of Fujian cooking is bounded on the rustic and practical. It says something about the relative penury of the province, and also its backwardness.

TYPICAL DISHES OF FUJIAN

Fujian cuisine is mostly peasant fare. Overall, the dishes are soupy, with sweet-and-sour flavors appearing frequently. Red fermented rice mash plays a pivotal role; it is the defining condiment of this cooking style.

Fuzhou-style Fun Soup
鍋邊糊

Leftover rice syrup (used to make fun) was once scraped from the sides of the pot to create irregular-sized sheets of rice noodles. These are then cooked in a soup flavored with dried scallops, dried shrimp, and whatever else is in the kitchen. It can be eaten as an appetizer, but mostly it is enough as a heart-warming meal in itself.

Rice vermicelli (Fengan)
粉干

There are rice vermicelli, and then there are rice vermicelli. Confused? Different regions have different ways of making rice vermicelli, and they all go by different names. A popular Fujian type is called "fengan." It is quite thick, almost like regular wheat noodles. Sometimes it is called "white noodles" because of its appearance.

Fuzhou-style Meatballs (Yanwan)
燕丸

They look like wontons, but don't be fooled. The wrappers are not made of flour but meat. Fish and pork fat are pounded into paste, and used to make this distinctive pork-filled meatball. Served in a soup, yanwan have a crunchy texture that is both sublime and unusual.

Fuzhou-style Fish balls (Yuwan)
福州魚丸

Fish balls can be found throughout southern China. Fish fillets are pounded until they become a pliable paste, which is then shaped to the size of golf balls. In Fuzhou, they stuff a tincture of seasoned ground pork inside.

Lychee Pork
荔枝肉

The dish gets its name because the meat looks like fresh lychees. Using ketchup as the basis of the marinade, pieces of pork are bright red after deep-frying with corn starch. The pieces are then braised in light broth with sugar and vinegar, resulting in the sweet-and-sour flavor typical of Fujian cuisine.

Buddha Jumping Over the Wall
佛跳牆

A hearty stew that could sometimes include 20 ingredients, it is said that a Buddhist monk once found the scents of it so irresistible that he jumped over a wall to taste it. The main ingredients include fish maw, dried scallops, and dried shrimp. Other ingredients are selected based on the whim of the chef. In Hongkong-style seafood houses, this dish often shows up with considerably more pomp – with delicacies such as shark's fin or abalone.

Crab Egg-fuyung
蟹抱蛋

Although seafood is abundant in Fujian cuisine, none is really a stellar standout. Crab egg-fuyung is quite interesting, however. Pieces of crab, with the shells intact, are stir-fried with scrambled eggs. This kind of egg-fuyung can also be used on fish, clams, and conch. Downright homey, you won't find anything like this in a Hongkong-style seafood house.

Conch dishes
海螺

Fujian cuisine uses considerably more saltwater conch. It is the peasant's abalone, having a similar chewy texture. On the Fujian menu, you can always expect to find conch cooked in the red rice wine mash. It can also be sautéed with fermented black beans, or simply boiled in water.

Braised Chicken in Red Rice Wine Mash
爆糟丁

With the red rice wine mash as the main condiment, this dish looks like a reddish chicken curry, with an unforgettably earthy flavor very typical of Fujian cooking. This cooking technique can be used on all sorts of meats. In restaurants, it is sometimes described as meats braised in Foo Chow (Fuzhou) sauce.

Red Rice Wine Mash Eel Fritters
紅糟鰻魚

The red rice wine mash is used to marinate the eel sections. The pieces are then battered and deep-fried to a crisp. It is a strong-flavored dish good either as an appetizer or for snacking with drinking buddies.

Little Fuzhou, New York

WHERE TO EAT FUJIAN IN THE BAY AREA

In China, few Fujian restaurants exist outside the province. New York is an exception, where in the past decade over 100,000 Fujian immigrants transformed Lower Manhattan east of the old Chinatown into a "Little Fuzhou" (the provincial capital). It is an immigrant wave mirroring the arrival of Guangdong immigrants in San Francisco during the 1860s. In that part of New York, Fujian restaurants far outnumber traditional Guangdong takeouts. The Bay Area, however, has so far been left completely out of the Fujian action.

台山同鄉會 **Toish**

Associa

台山
同鄉
會

Oakland Chinatown

Dabing and mantou

Northern China

If Chinese food had a fly-over country, then northern China must be it. Much maligned by the rest of China, the food of the north is a dullard in a land of colorful regional cuisines. Yet, the north has nevertheless maintained a mysterious allure around itself, tucking in some interesting gems that stand out above the daily monotony of Napa cabbage, leeks, and *shaobing* that dominate the average northern meal.

The cooking style of Shandong province best represents the cuisine of northern China. Located north of China's Rice-Wheat Line, the main diet of Shandong is based on wheat, barley, millet, and other rough grains. Noodles, pastries, and breads of all sorts are consumed with hardly any rice in the staple. Beijing, the Chinese capital, actually does not have much of a cuisine to call its own. Its cooking style is heavily influenced by Shandong. Beijing does have, however, the world-famous Beijing duck. Northern China is also the home to Islamic-Chinese cuisine, as well as the Mongolian hotpot.

For the most part, northern Chinese cuisine is practical and simple. Generations of hardship shaped this cuisine that is mostly concerned with frugality and survival. Aside from the wheat-based diet, which is wholly different from the rest of China, the northern cuisine is also a testament to the Chinese experience – a compact history of a civilization interlaced with disasters, sufferings, and triumphs through time.

SHANDONG CUISINE

Shandong's climate is similar to the Northern Plains of the U.S., which is well suited for growing grains such as barley, corn, millet, sorghum, and wheat. Unlike the rest of China, breads and noodles are the important staples of the region. Rice does not grow there, so the local diet defies the common stereotype that Chinese are rice-eating people. It is not unusual for a northerner to eat rice only a few times a year, if at all.

Among the vegetables, nothing is as dominant as the Napa cabbage – often called Chinese cabbage. In the warm but short growing season, a variety of summer vegetables like greens, legumes, and squash are harvested. These short months provide a welcomed deviation from nonstop Napa, which the entire north basically subsists upon during the cold winter months.

The silt-laden waters of the Yellow River are not conducive to much freshwater fish. However, good quality seafood is plentiful along the coast. The most notable seafood items include abalone and sea cucumbers. Overall, the variety of fish and seafood in Shandong cuisine lags far behind Jiangzhe and Guangdong cuisines. It also does not generate as much excitement as the other two.

TYPICAL SHANDONG DISHES

Shandong cuisine is practical and simple – resorting mainly to techniques that save fuel and cooking fat. Flavorings of Shandong dishes do not venture too far from three primarily condiments: salt, vinegar, and the sweet bean paste. There are hardly any hot or spicy dishes to speak of. However, foreign influences exist, most significantly from the Arabs and Mongolians of centuries past. Many Shandong dishes are boiled in large pots, bringing it a step closer to Korean cooking. And almost invariably, many of these boiled dishes feature the ubiquitous Napa cabbage.

Kaiyang Napa
開洋白菜

Napa cabbage is the most important vegetable in northern Chinese cuisine, and this dish is probably the most famous of them all. Napa cabbage is braised with dried shrimp and mushroom in a light broth, and boiled down to a soft and tender consistency. The cooking liquid turns into a flavorful broth and is fully absorbed into the Napa itself.

Napa Cabbage in Vinegar Sauce
醋溜白菜

A different way of braising Napa cabbage is to cook it in white or rice vinegar and broth. Sometimes, white tree fungus is added to provide a crunchy contrast to the dish. This dish has strong ties to Shanxi province, where nearly all the local dishes are sour, flavored with vinegar.

Fish Braised in Vinegar Sauce
醋溜魚片

The braising technique above can also be applied to meats and seafood. Fish, pork, and tripe are all common ingredients.

Flash-fried Beef with Pickled Napa
酸菜爆牛肉

Northern China has its own sauerkraut. It is an entire head of Napa cabbage preserved with salt and vinegar. A simple flash-fry like this one shows how the pickled Napa is an important condiment in local cooking, which is often sour-flavored. Lamb is a regular alternative to beef in this dish.

Dry-sautéed Green Beans
干扁四季豆

Dry sautéing involves flash-frying the vegetables inside a covered wok, using only oil and no liquid. This way, the natural textures and colors of the green beans are not cooked down. After removing the green beans from the pan, the skins cool off and contract to create attractive wrinkles that give the dish its interesting appeal.

Shredded Pork Flash-fried in Sweet Bean Paste
京醬肉絲

This is also called Beijing-style pork. The sweet bean paste is also called "Beijing Sauce," and has an immediate association with northern China. This is a typical home-style dish that is an ideal accompaniment to breads and congee.

Chop-suey with a Hat on Top
合菜戴帽

An assortment of flash-fried vegetables (hecai) includes the northern favorites of bean sprouts, black tree fungus, yellow nira, bamboo shoot, and carrots. Shredded pork, dried tofu and cellophane noodles are sometimes added to make an opulent chop-suey. A thin sheet of grilled scrambled eggs is layered on top, like a hat, to complete the dish.

Dalu Mian
打鲁麵

The most famous noodle dish from Shandong is just a bowl of noodles served in a starchy egg-drop soup. Any variety of ingredients can go into the soup, but a typical northern Chinese soup includes Napa, mushrooms, and leeks. This simple but hearty dish says much about Shandong cuisine, which relies on noodles and soups to endure the long winters.

Fish Fillet Braised in Fermented Rice Sauce
糟溜魚片

The fermented rice sauce is made from fermented rice wine mash, which has a sweet and grainy flavor. This is not the red mash used in Fujian cuisine, but the white ones used throughout China. The rice wine mash used to create the sauce does not overwhelm the delicate flavors of the fish; instead it adds light and refreshing aromas and flavors.

Pan-fried Tofu Squares
鍋塌豆腐

Square pieces of tofu are coated with egg wash and flour, and pan-fried until golden brown. Then, they are simmered in a clear broth until all of the cooking liquids are absorbed into the tofu. The dish, albeit simple, transforms the otherwise bland pieces of tofu into savory, nutrition-packed gems.

Candied Flossing
拔絲

An attempt at dessert making, this is the Shandong answer to caramel apples. Sugar is caramelized with oil in a wok, and then coated onto deep-fried fruits: typically apple, taro, or yam. The action that follows must happen lightning fast. When you pick up a piece with chopsticks, the sugar is pulled to form thin strands of flossing around the fruit. Then dip the piece into an ice bath, which hardens the sugar into a crunchy candy coating. If you move too slowly, the candy hardens right onto the plate.

Soups

Shandong cuisine makes use of a lot of soups. It generally starts with one of two basic types of stock: a clear broth and a milk broth. The "clear broth" is made by slowly simmering meat bones. A "milk broth" is produced by boiling the same kinds of meat bones over high heat and for longer periods. No milk is used in the milk broth, although it comes out looking like a creamy consistency. The duck soup served at the end of a Beijing duck "eaten three ways" meal is a fine example of this milk broth (see next page).

BEIJING DUCK

Beijing duck is a 600-year old tradition. It was favored by past emperors and loved by the modern-day masses. Today, Beijing duck is singularly the dish of the city, and it is the most popular duck in the world. Even Wolfgang Puck, an Austrian-born Provençal chef in Los Angeles, has found a way to put Beijing duck on his pizzas.

Preparing Beijing duck is a tedious process that takes a better part of the day. For instance, the duck must be air dried for several hours so that the skin could become very crispy. Also, air must be pumped into the skin, and boiling broth poured into the sealed body cavity, before the roasting process begins.

Even though you can find "Peking Duck" in nearly every Chinese restaurant, almost no one does things the authentic way. Most are prepared in advance and deep-fried just before serving to simulate the crispy skin. For that reason, you are actually eating "twice-cooked" duck.

The traditional way of eating Beijing duck is called "One Duck Eaten Three Ways". Duck skin is served first as an appetizer, eaten either with steamed lotus leaf-like buns, or shaobing. They are wrapped together with slices of fresh leeks or scallions, smeared with a daub of sweet bean paste. The duck meat – without the skins – is served next as the main course. Commonly, the duck meat is stir-fried with bean sprouts and duck fat. Another popular vegetable to stir-fry with is yellow nira. Lastly, a milky soup made from duck bones is served after the meal. This is a traditional Shandong-style soup, which attains the milky consistency by boiling the bones over high heat.

Noodle-making

Shandong chefs are master noodle makers. In a cuisine based wholly on wheat, inventive ways of using wheat flour have become artistic skills. In Shandong cuisine, the variety of noodles is bewildering. Commonly known types of noodles include Knife-cut Noodles, Yi-fu Mein, and Cat's Ears (See separate chapter on Dumplings & Noodles).

NORTHERN

Noodle factory

WHERE TO EAT SHANDONG IN THE BAY AREA

Shandong restaurants offer a nonstop bonanza of breads and Napa. Wholesome peasant fare is the norm, so don't expect haute cuisine. However, some of Shandong's finest dishes are among the most famous in all of Chinese cooking, so sampling these dishes opens new vistas to the Chinese eating culture.

The Bay Area is shortchanged on much of this adventure. Shandong restaurants, in the strictest sense, are non-existent. Whatever northern Chinese food that exists comes in the form of dumplings & noodle shops and Islamic-Chinese restaurants (see next chapters).

ISLAMIC-CHINESE CUISINE

A curious aspect of Chinese cuisine is the cooking style following strict Islamic dietary laws. China has a small but visible Muslim minority, with about 10 million people called the *Hui*. That is just under 1 percent of the total population, but their cuisine is quite popular with all Chinese. Muslim presence in China dates back to about 750 A.D., when Arab and Persian traders first arrived in the ports of southern China. Faithful to their religion, the Huis adhere to the *halal* diet. Their style of cooking, called Islamic-Chinese cuisine, is in essence Shandong cuisine with the Koran and a few other surprises thrown in.

For one, the Koran outlines specific foods deemed "lawful" for consumption – or *halal*. These laws reveal the ways by which Muslims select, prepare, and eat food. Among the foods expressly forbidden by the Koran – or *haram* – is pork. Other haram foods include crustaceans such as clams, crabs, and shrimp. Also, alcohol is completely banned: beers, wines, and liquors play no role in the Muslim diet, either as a beverage or as an ingredient in cooking.

Another major difference of Islamic-Chinese cuisine is the type of meats used. Instead of pork, Islamic-Chinese dishes frequently feature beef and lamb. This is unlike the Hans, who rarely eat beef or lamb.

Like Shandong, the main staple of Islamic-Chinese cuisine is based on wheat. *Dabing*, or "big pancake," is the basic bread in Islamic-Chinese meals. Similar to shaobing, its diminutive brethren, dabing is eaten to accompany all sorts of dishes. It is the size of a large pizza – up to sixteen inches in diameter and around two inches thick. Some are covered with roasted white sesame seeds. Noodles are also popular, mirroring Shandong's noodle-making traditions.

TYPICAL DISHES OF ISLAMIC-CHINESE CUISINE

Notable with Islamic-Chinese restaurants is the abundance of lamb dishes. Also, any Islamic-Chinese meal cannot be complete without dabing, which is always eaten instead of rice, so always plan to order one for the table.

Dabing, Shaobing
芝麻大餅, 燒餅

A large, grilled sesame pancake, or dabing, is about the size of a Chicago-style deep-dish pizza, while shaobing is the shape of a business-size envelope. Both are eaten like bread to accompany all meals. A dabing is ample for six to eight people, while the smaller shaobing is an individual serving. Some people prefer eating these pancakes flavored with scallions or leeks.

Pancakes in a Lamb Soup
羊肉泡饃

This is the ultimate frugal food of northern China. A piece of dabing is dunked under a bowl of lamb (or beef) soup, sopping up all of its juices and flavors. This is not unlike the French who soak their day-old baguettes in soups to avoid waste.

Knife-cut Noodles
刀削麵

A northern Chinese specialty, these broad, flat noodles are sliced from a ball of dough. The rough, uneven texture of these noodles suggests the ruggedness of the northern terrain. They are best served with a lamb- or beef-soup. Stir-fried is also not bad.

Flash-fried Lamb with Leeks

蔥爆羊肉

This is perhaps the signature Islamic-Chinese dish.
Thin slices of lamb are flash-fried in very hot oil
with chopped leeks. Flash-frying cooks faster than
stir-frying and uses less oil. This dish goes very
well with dabing, making it a very simple and
inexpensive meal. Beef is a common substitute for
lamb in this dish.

Grilled Lamb with Cumin

孜然羊肉

The flavor of cumin is atypical for Chinese cooking.
The Chinese generally avoid it like vampires
scattering to the scent of garlic. Islamic-Chinese
restaurants are the few places where this dish can
be found. Grilled lamb, seasoned with cumin and
served in a kabob, gives an unmistakable aura of
Central Asia and the Middle East.

Splitting a dabing

WHERE TO EAT ISLAMIC-CHINESE IN THE BAY AREA

Islamic-Chinese cuisine is often overshadowed by more flamboyant cuisines from other parts of China. But people routinely seek them out for their sheer novelty. Look around inside an Islamic-Chinese restaurant and you will find all kinds of people: Americans, Malaysians, Pakistanis, and Chinese, dining together with their families and friends. Unfortunately, most restaurants feel they also have to pomp their menus with seafood, "Peking" duck, and familiar takeout dishes in order to keep business going. Feel free to skip them. For the genuine Islamic-Chinese experience, stick with the coarse repertory of dabing, noodles, and Shandong-style flash-fries.

Fatima Seafood Restaurant
清真馬家海鮮館

The menu drifts aimlessly to embrace non-halal dishes, such as shrimp and sea cucumbers. They can be easily overlooked if you concentrate on the beef and lamb dishes instead; they occupy about half the menu here. Instead of rice, get either the thin pancake or the thicker dabing (sesame "bread" here). Also the knife-cut noodles ("soft noodle") are a house specialty.

1132 De Anza Blvd., #A, San Jose

408.257.3893
11.00 – 21.30

Also at:

1208 S. El Camino Real, San Mateo
650.554.1818
11.00 – 21.30

Mastercard, Visa

Ma's Restaurant
清真馬家館

The restaurant proclaims its menu as "Islamic and Mandarin Cuisines," and that is an instant sign of trouble. ("Mandarin" cuisine does not exist.) Even the endless parade of beef and lamb appears as haphazard attempts at legitimizing "kungpao," "twice-cooked," and "sweet-and-sour."

Even though the extent of Islamic-Chinese dishes easily fits on a 3x5, sticking with this handful of authentic classics is enough to bring people back for more.

1715 Lundy Ave., #168, San Jose
408.437.2499
11.00 – 21.30

Mastercard, Visa

Old Mandarin Islamic Restaurant
老北京

The old Beijinger serves up a homey mix of northern and Islamic dishes that characterize Beijing's local cuisine. Try some of the snacks, like a sesame pancake stuffed with beef sautéed in sweet bean paste ("Peking beef pie"). Knife-cut noodles and cat's ears (see page 109) are egalitarian answers to Guangdong's chow mein.

3132 Vincente St., San Francisco (Sunset)
415.564.3481
11.30 – 21.30, at 17.30 on Tuesdays

Mastercard, Visa

DUMPLINGS & NOODLES

Wheat is the most important food staple of northern China. Many northerners eat noodles, pancakes and dumplings three times a day, and may go for days without eating rice. Similar to the local diet, northern-style restaurants serve all kinds of wheat-based foods with nary a rice dish on their menus. This is the primary attraction of the dumplings & noodles houses, which serve exactly just that – dumplings and noodles.

Dumpling & noodle houses are also known for their breakfasts, a rarity among other Chinese restaurants. Besides the wheat-based foods, these restaurants serve a host of dishes comprised of grains such as barley, millet, and oats – the typical roughage for the north. These foods are fortifying enough for the cold, and packed with ample nutrition to get through the day.

CHINESE BREAKFASTS

For the most part, Chinese breakfasts are an acquired taste. In a culture with such rich culinary traditions, it is nearly inexplicable that the Chinese could make such poor breakfasts. But they do. With the exception of Guangdong (and Hongkong), the Chinese breakfast is unimaginative, bland, and rather unhealthy. The list of perennial losers on the breakfast menu includes such uninspiring deadweights as a soggy nira pancake deep-fried in oil, a flavorless bowl of congee, and a leaden glutinous rice ball stuffed with fried pork and chopped *zhacai* (see page 127).

The most notorious breakfast item is *youtiao*, or loosely translated as the "oil stick." Some also call it a cruller. It is nothing more than a greasy rod of deep-fried flour dough. Its mass appeal makes it the Chinese rebuttal to Krispy Kreme. Youtiao can be eaten like a donut by dunking into soymilk, or sandwiched between a *shaobing* like a breakfast meat. Some people chop up the leftovers to use as croutons over hot soy milk.

The customary breakfast beverage is soymilk, which the Chinese eat hot or cold, and flavored salty or sweet. Hot soymilk can be seasoned with soy sauce, or sweetened by adding sugar. In either case, hot soymilk is always served in a bowl, and eaten like a soup with a spoon. On the other hand, cold soymilk is always served sweet, and drunk as a beverage from a glass.

NORTHERN

TYPICAL DUMPLINGS & NOODLES HOUSE DISHES

Soymilk Gelatin (douhua)
豆花

Also called variously by the names soy brain, soy flower, tofu "fa", or the Mandarin pronunciation "douhua" – soymilk gelatin is made by adding edible plaster to soymilk. When allowed to coagulate, it forms into a flimsy solid that is softer than tofu. It is eaten like a custard, either hot or cold. Cold gelatin is always served sweet, with hot sugar syrup poured on top. Fanciful garnishes include green beans, lotus seeds, and even boba. Hot gelatin can be served either sweet or salty. In the latter case, it is seasoned with soy sauce, chili oil, and even youtiao as croutons.

Xiaolongbao (Soupy dumplings)
小籠湯包子

Call them however you want: soupy bao, soup dumplings, or even by the initials X.L.B. (for the Mandarin pronunciation *xiaolongbao*). These gems are served in little steamer baskets, each containing eight or ten bite-sized baozi. They are very juicy, and should be eaten with chopsticks in one hand and spoon in the other. Bite into the baozi carefully to release a torrent of hot, savory soup into the spoon. Pop the whole thing into your mouth and you may need a lawyer to heal your pains. A small dish of shredded ginger is always provided. Add vinegar, soy sauce, and a dash of sugar for a light dipping sauce to go along.

Potstickers
鍋貼

Sometimes called "fried dumplings," potstickers start out as raw jiaozi in a shallow pan. Over heat, they are first browned on the bottom with oil. Then, water is added, which steams the upper half. When all the water has evaporated, the top is soft and chewy, and the bottom is crunchy.

Longevity Peach
壽桃

A specialty baozi served only on birthdays, longevity peach is a heart-shaped bun that looks like a white-fleshed peach. Longevity peach is filled with sweet black sesame paste, and the outside flour shell is daubed with red food coloring to simulate the appearance of a peach. Trendy longevity peach now comes with fillings such as mashed lotus seeds, date paste, and even pumpkin. Since they are typically eaten on birthdays, these are rarely sold retail. Order them from a dumpling house or bakery.

OTHER BREADS OF NORTHERN CHINA

The standard "breads" of northern China are the ubiquitous mantou and shaobing. Dabing, or the "big pancake," is also universally popular. A lesser known bread, the "wowotou," is the waif of Chinese cookery that even northerners eagerly disavow. Pancakes, which are fried dough made of high-gluten flour, are popular street snacks throughout China that have found new homes on the menus of nearly every dumpling & noodle houses in North America.

Dabing, Shaobing
大餅, 燒餅

These grilled pancakes vary in size. A dabing is big enough for an entire family, while shaobing is much like a personal-sized baguette. Sesame and scallions are usually the only variations to these plain breads. See page 99.

BAOZI AND JIAOZI

Baozi are round dumplings encapsulating a variety of meat and vegetable fillings. The flour wraps can be either thick or thin; leavened or unleavened. Leavened flour wraps become fluffy when steamed, because of the baking soda used. Guangdong-style baozi are generally leavened this way, and are also sweetened with a pinch of sugar. Northern-style baozi use both leavened and unleavened wraps, but are generally *sans* sugar. Shanghai is famous for its *xiaolongbao*, or "small steamer-basket baozi," which uses unleavened wraps to create a watertight package to hold in the soup inside.

A baozi is shaped by pinching the flour wrap in a circular fashion, creating pillow-like contours around the filling. The little dimples on top are its main characteristic. Mostly, baozi are steamed. They can also be pan-fried in a covered frying pan. A pan-fried xiaolongbao is called shenjianbao. Baozi are never boiled.

Jiaozi use only thin and unleavened flour wraps. Fillings for jiaozi can also be of any variety of meats and vegetables. The wrap is pinched in a linear fashion, creating an oblong-shaped dumpling. The most common way to cook them is by boiling, but steaming is becoming increasingly popular. Jiaozi can also be pan-fried, in which case they are called *potstickers*. On the streets, you can also find them simply as "fried dumplings." The Japanese eat *gyoza*, which is actually just their way of pronouncing the word jiaozi.

Unlike baozi, which can be eaten plain, jiaozi are always eaten with some sort of dipping sauce. The most basic is plain soy sauce. More elaborate sauces can be made by combining soy sauce with any of the following: sugar, vinegar, garlic, fresh chili peppers, fermented chili bean paste, sesame oil, and garlic. In northern China, some people like to eat boiled jiaozi with alternating bites into fresh leeks or garlic cloves.

Mantou
饅頭

Dabing, shaobing, and mantou are the Three Musketeers of Chinese breads. Literally the "savage's head," mantou is just a steamed lump of leavened flour dough. According to legend, primitive Chinese once offered human heads in sacrificial rituals. When the civilization prevailed with cooler heads, mantou became the more practical alternative. Today, they come in such designer colors as purple from taro starch, brown from whole wheat, yellow from cornmeal, and even green by adding green tea.

Wowotou
窩窩頭

This classic northern bread is made from corn meal. Wowotou has a distinctive cone shape, which, after steaming, is golden brown in color. The dry, flaky texture is quite different from other steamed breads, which are chewier and moister. Detractors of wowotou liken its consistency to leavened sawdust. Likewise, many Chinese quickly associate wowotou with famine, because it is often perceived as the food of the last resort.

Mantou

Fried Scallion Pancakes

油餅

Scallion pancakes are flat, round pastries the size of a tea saucer. High gluten flour is kneaded with hot water so that it becomes a highly stretchable dough that can be pulled apart without breaking. The dough is also leavened with baking soda so it becomes fluffy when fried. Many people add an egg to the pancake during the pan-frying process, making it a handy breakfast item for those on the run.

Youtiao

油條

High gluten flour is leavened with baking soda and saltpeter to make the dough so stretchable that a thin strand of it swells to ten times the size when deep-fried in hot oil. Youtiao is a crunchy, airy "stick" that is mostly hollow on the inside. Some people dip it into a bowl of hot soymilk, just like how donuts are dunked into coffee.

NOODLES

Not all noodles are created equal. Many of the north's favorites, such as Shandong's hand-pulled noodles, require special skills. Neighboring Shanxi province is renowned for several types of noodles, such as knife-cut noodles and "cat's ears."

Hand-pulled Noodles

拉麵

A Shandong specialty, hand-pulling noodles requires a certain degree of dexterity and acrobatic skill. From a single ball of dough, the chef gradually kneads and pulls the noodles into long, sinewy strands that can reach more than twenty feet in length. Long noodles symbols of longevity, so hand-pulled noodles are typically served at birthday banquets, most typically for a person's 80th birthday.

Knife-cut Noodles

刀削麵

This Shanxi specialty is shaved with a knife from a single ball of dough. Its uneven texture is the primary attraction to this noodle, which is thin around the edges and thick near the center. Knife-cut noodles can be used just like other noodles – served as a stir-fry or in soups.

"Cat's Ears"
貓耳朵

Pieces of flour dough are flattened into a thin disk the size of a penny, and then pressed by the thumb to create small, curled pasta shaped like cat's ears. This noodle is very similar to the Italian orecchiétte, and has some resemblance to Spätzle as well. Cat's ears are used just like any other type of noodles: in noodle soups, stir-fries, or served like pasta with some sort of sauce made from an assortment of meats and vegetables.

Beef Noodle Soup
牛肉麵

Beef Noodle Soup is the gold standard among all other Chinese noodle soups. The favorite type is the Sichuan's numbing-hot beef soup, which later became popularized in Taiwan's street snack scene. A non-spicy "red-cooked" beef soup is also popular.

Beef noodle soup

Making egg-roll flour wrappers

WHERE TO HAVE DUMPLINGS & NOODLES IN THE BAY AREA

Dumplings & noodles houses have flourished lately, thanks to the arrival of northerners who crave for the rice-less diet like they had back home. Among the most important "dumplings" in the northern diet are baozi, jiaozi, and shaobing. Noodles run the gamut from thin hair-like strands to broad, knife-cut noodles. Many of these places also serve the traditional Chinese breakfast, which are an eye-opener in more ways than one.

House of Noodles
老鄒麵館

Mr. Zou is a northerner; you can tell by his rare last name. The noodles are made in-house, including ones called "jade" (green from spinach) and "coral" (orange from carrots). Beef noodle soups include the mala (numbing-hot) Sichuan-style, a clear broth, and one seasoned with five-spice. Dalu mian (called "combination noodle soup with egg" here) is a good heart-warmer. The rest of the menu features an array of pan-China stir-fries that may or may not tempt your curiosity. The soymilk-based breakfast is served on weekend mornings.

690 Barber Ln., Milpitas
408.321.8838
11.00 – 21.30

Cash only

Fortune Garden
一品香

Hand-pulled noodles are served here. Ask whether they have them on hand because it is not always available. Boiled jiaozi, xiaolongbao, and potstickers round out the mix of ordinary but well made staples. On weekends, the menu expands to include several vegetarian (using kaofu) noodle soups.

1773 Decoto Rd., Union City
510.487.9168
11.30 – 21.00, closed Tuesday

Cash only

Café Yulong
玉龍小館

Even the takeout dishes here are done nicely to make a special trip worthwhile, but concentrate on the "fresh house made noodles." The family recipe traveled here from Shandong via Korea, Taiwan, and the North Shore of suburban Chicago. Especially noteworthy are the fish and leek (nira actually) dumplings. They are difficult to make because of the moisture content involved, so you won't find them elsewhere – or at least made as well as they are here.

743 W. Dana St., Mountain View
650.960.1677
11.30 – 21.30, until 22.30 on weekends

All credit cards

Sun Tung Restaurant
山東小館

The "home-made specials" are the boiled jiaozi, which come in an ordinary pork filling, as well as a rather exotic filling of dill and minced shrimp. Xiaolongbao and stir-fried rice cakes round out the extent of noteworthy dishes to try. Also try the "tai-roo noodle soup," which is dalu mian (see page 92).

153 S. B St., San Mateo
650.342.5330
11.30 – 21.00, at 10.30 on weekends. Closed Monday

Mastercard, Visa

The Pot Sticker
爐京

The place calls itself "Mandarin" cuisine, and takes pains to explain what it is (even though there is no such thing as Mandarin cuisine). This is for the tourists, and so are the scads of stir-fries that serve as distractions to the real gems here: the "dim sum" section on the menu. There you will find northern-style dumplings, like xiaolongboa/shenjianbao, potstickers, and scallion pancakes. The "family flower cake" is a flaky pancake that pulls apart easily into thin strands of dough. The boiled jiaozi come in a variety of fillings like chicken, nira, and shrimp. Stick with these and you will have a completely different dining experience.

150 Waverly Pl., Chinatown
415.397.9985
11.00 – 22.00

Mastercard, Visa

MONGOLIAN HOTPOT

Hotpots are cook-it-yourself meals: meats, vegetables, and a large variety of ingredients are cooked in the boiling broth inside the hotpot. Meats are sliced thinly, to around an eighth of an inch thickness. Just about any kind of meat can be used: lamb, beef, pork, chicken, and fish. Others such as tripe, liver, and kidney offer additional possibilities. Among the vegetables are the hotpot requisites: chrysanthemum leaves, Napa cabbage, and an assortment of mushrooms.

The physical hotpot itself is a unique cooking vessel. Old-school hotpot is a donut-shaped bowl set on a coal-burning chamber. A chimney rises from the center to allow smoke to float above people's faces. However, people less inclined to mess with coal these days, so they opt for the gas or electric tabletop stoves with an ordinary pot set on top instead. Either way, the hotpot should not be confused with the Mongolian barbecue. The latter is a buffet style free-for-all, in which people pile meats, vegetables, and seasonings on a plate for a communal stir-fry on a flat iron grill.

A good dipping sauce is essential to any good hotpotting. Generally, the Chinese like their dipping sauces thick and very strongly flavored, so they make them out of such ingredients as: sesame paste, nira paste, salted fermented tofu, fermented chili bean paste, soy sauce, garlic, scallions, and so forth.

Because each region has its own style of hotpot, the dipping sauces differ as well. In the north, the vinegary hotpot of pickled Napa calls for a sesame paste-based sauce flavored with nira paste. The numbing-hot hotpot of Sichuan, called *malaguo*, is already spicy enough so that it needs no additional dipping sauce. However, many still like a light sesame sauce to tame down some of its numbing-hotness. In Taiwan, a barbecue sauce made from bonito fish flakes is popular as the base of the dipping sauce.

Hotpot setup

WHERE TO EAT HOTPOTS IN THE BAY AREA

The Chinese prefer eating hotpots in the warmth and intimacy of their own homes. But hotpots with regional twists offer intrigue that draws regular followings to hotpot restaurants throughout town. Restaurants serving regional Chinese cuisines offer all sorts of hotpots with unusual broths and flavors. The numbing-hot malaguo once ruled the Chinese malls, but its domain is being challenged by the so-called Inner Mongolia hotpot, containing herbal Chinese medicine. To spot a restaurant serving hotpots, just look for Chinese diners hovering over a steaming hotpot on the table. It helps to ask about all the soup broths they have in the kitchen. Below are some of the special ones around town.

Coriya
可利亞

The all-you-can-eat buffet line is stocked with all the hotpot fixings you can imagine – from meats to seafood to fresh vegetables. You also make your own dipping sauce from a pantry-full of condiments. The specially-designed hotpot has flanged sides, which allow you to grill the food in addition to cooking in the broth.

3288 Pierce St., #A105, Richmond
510.524.8081
11.30 – 00.00

Mastercard, Visa

Another hotpot restaurant in Milpitas has the same Chinese name, but different owners. Its décor and service are similar:

Hot Pot City
可利亞

500 Barber Ln., Milpitas
408.428.0988
11.00 – 00.00, until 01.00 on weekends

Mastercard, Visa

Kingswood Teppan Steak House
上林鐵板燒餐廳

On one side is teppanyaki. On the other side the tables are outfitted for the Taiwan-style yuanyangguo hotpot, featuring a one-two punch of clear and numbing-hot broths. You just order the cuts of meats and vegetables, and cook away. The place is very popular with families, especially on weekends.

10935 N. Wolfe Rd., Cupertino
408.255.5928
11.30 - 22.30, until 00.00 on weekends

Mastercard, Visa

39055 Cedar Blvd., Newark
(opening September 2004)

Mastercard, Visa

Café Ophelia-Fremont
芳苑咖啡西餐

Various themed hotpots are served: broths flavored with pickled Napa (with "kimchi"), or numbing-hot (with "spicy sauce"). And following the current hotpot trend, there are also hotpots with a broth based on Chinese medicine ("herbal hotpot").

46801 Warm Springs Blvd., Fremont
510.668.0998
17.30 - 00.00

Mastercard, Visa

also at

516 Barber Ln., Milpitas
408.943.1020
11.30 – 22.00, until 00.00 on weekends

Mastercard, Visa

Ninji's Mala Hot Pot Restaurant
寧記麻辣火鍋

The house's specialty is the numbing-hot malaguo. You can choose to have it straight up, or as yuanyang (combination) alongside a clear broth. Choose the cooking ingredients from an order blank on the table. Nothing is complicated about venturing into this aspect of Chinese eating culture.

6066 Mowry Ave., Newark
510.792.2898
11.30 – 22.00

Mastercard, Visa

Fook Yuen Seafood Restaurant
馥苑海鲜酒家

The seafood palace is an institution for banquets, but it also serves a mean series of seafood hotpots. You can choose between a clear broth and a spicy "Szechwan" broth. There is also a prepared Dungeness crab hotpot, with cellophane noodles and other fixings already arranged and bubbling when brought to the table.

195 El Camino Real, Millbrae
650.692.8600
17.30 – 21.30

All credit cards

Old Mandarin Islamic Restaurant
老北京

The northern-style hotpot features a clear, light broth. You can choose to have it flavored with pickled Napa or without. Lamb is the obligatory meat of choice, but no one will snicker if you go with beef. Fixings for the dipping sauce include sesame paste and a pungent nira sauce.

3132 Vincente St., San Francisco (Sunset)
415.564.3481
11.30 – 21.30, at 17.30 on Tuesdays

Mastercard, Visa

WESTERN CHINA

China's most popular and creative cuisine comes from the "Heavenly Kingdom" – as Sichuan (Szechwan) province is commonly known. Sichuan is an isolated province located in the blessed western part of China, surrounded by tall, misty mountains and swift-flowing rivers. Free from many of the warfare and famines that plagued the rest of China, Sichuan developed a mind of its own with everything it does. Its cuisine, supported by a fertile land that produces three rice crops a year, stands alone for a single characteristic: the numbing-hot flavor. It is a strange and strangely mystifying sensation that is unmatched by anything else in this world.

Sichuan cuisine is the dominant force in the cooking of western China, but a few distinctive dishes exist from Sichuan's neighbors. Yunnan province, located to the southwest of Sichuan, is known for a dish called Across the Bridge Rice Noodles, and a curious cooking vessel called the airpot. Guizhou, a poor province to the southeast, is credited for gracing the world with Gongbao (Kungpao) chicken. The rest of Yunnan and Guizhou's cuisines are awash with mediocrity.

For a long time, restaurateurs and chefs were afraid to offer authentic Sichuan cuisine. Americans accustomed to Chinese takeouts generally find Sichuan's fiery red dishes to be a shock to their palates. The Guangdong people, who have long shaped the image of Chinese food in America, can also barely tolerate it. However, as more people seek out the real Sichuan, chefs are increasingly emboldened to unleash what is arguably the best and most complex cuisine China has to offer.

SICHUAN CUISINE

Sichuan dishes are known to be fiery, flamboyant, and fragrant. They are certainly not for the timid. Most attractive about it is the complex flavors constructed from an ingenious use of ingredients. It is the regional style the Chinese love most. Dishes like gongbao (kungpao) chicken, twice-cooked pork, and hot-and-sour soup are household names in China. In America, these dishes also appear in takeout restaurants all over Main Street.

Sichuan cuisine employs a dizzying array of condiments and spices. The most well known among them are star anise, fermented chili-bean paste, *zhacai* (see separate section), chili powder, pickled chili, lily buds, black tree fungus, black vinegar, and Sichuan peppercorns. From them, Sichuan chefs created many unique flavors unheard of elsewhere: "Strange-flavor Chicken" uses five different spices, "Lychee-flavor Beef" uses no lychees at all, and "Fish-flavor Eggplant" is purely vegetarian.

The flavors constructed from chili peppers can be so varied that the Sichuan people have different ways of describing their hotness. Like the Eskimos have a hundred ways of describing "snow," Sichuan has "dry-hot" dishes by stir-frying dried chili or chili powder; "wet-hot" dishes from the use of fermented chili paste; "sour-hot" flavors from blending black rice vinegar with ground white pepper; and "numbing-hot" dishes from the combination of chili peppers with the legendary Sichuan peppercorns.

DO YOU CHENGDU? OR SHALL WE CHONGQING?

There are two primary divisions of Sichuan cuisine. They revolve around Sichuan's two major cities – Chengdu and Chongqing.

Chengdu, the provincial capital, is known for its street-snacking culture. Throughout the city, snack vendors line the streets and alleys, serving bite-sized snacks on the go. Many vendors invented their own snack dishes – noodles, pastries, and small meat dishes. Many of these became quite famous and are now served in restaurants.

Chongqing, a major industrial city on the Yangtze, has for centuries attracted migrants from the surrounding countryside. Chongqing's cuisine reflects the peasant heritage of those migrants, with some added big-city refinements. Some say that Chongqing's flavors are hotter than Chengdu's dishes. Chengdu supporters counter by claiming their dishes are more flavorful. This has opened the way to another unresolved sibling rivalry, further complicating the world.

TYPICAL SICHUAN DISHES

Many dishes in Sichuan cuisine have strange-sounding names equaling their unique flavors. Some are also fabled legends. All it takes to begin the adventure are a little curiosity, some courage, and lots of ice water.

Gongbao (Kungpao) Chicken
宮保雞丁

This is a so-called lychee-flavored dish, which relies on a dash of *Zhenjiang* black vinegar for a slightly tart, fruity flavor suggestive of eating a fresh lychee. Traditionally, gongbao chicken consists only of diced chicken, peanuts, and slivers of dried chili. Green peppers are sometimes added. When the Guangdong immigrants brought the recipe to America in the late 1800s, they altered it by using things like plum sauce and pineapples. Often the peanuts are skipped altogether.

Chongqing-style Chili with Chicken
重慶辣子雞

To call it "chicken with chili" would be a misnomer. There are more chilies than chicken in this dish (at least it appears that way). Equal amounts of whole dried red chili and diced chicken are stir-fried with Sichuan peppercorns. A dash of soy sauce enhances the numbing-hot punch of this simple dish. Beer is the perfect beverage and antidote to the thuggish hotness that envelopes the palate.

PEPPERCORNS ÜBER ALLES

People think chili peppers define Sichuan cuisine, but it is actually the Sichuan peppercorn (pinyin: huajiao) that sets it apart from all the rest. Sichuan peppercorns resemble ordinary black peppercorns in size and appearance, but they taste nothing like them. In fact, Sichuan peppercorns are not peppercorns actually, but are the fruit berries of a prickly ash tree (*pimpinella anisum*) that grows in the temperate mountain climates of China, Japan and North America. While the Chinese and Japanese varieties are edible (the Japanese call theirs *sansho*), only the Sichuan ones impart a peculiarly numbing sensation akin to kissing a 9-volt battery (with a more pleasant result).

When Sichuan peppercorns are combined with chili peppers, the chili pepper's hotness not only tastes hotter, it leaps with a lingering dryness and numbing sensation. The Chinese call this flavor "numbing-hot," and they go crazy for it. Because Sichuan peppercorns cannot grow elsewhere, the numbing-hot flavor is a sole Sichuan propriety. Whoever wants to emulate the numbing-hot flavor must have the peppercorns imported.

Unfortunately, the U.S. Food and Drug Administration bans the importation of fresh Sichuan peppercorns. They are believed to carry a tree blight that attacks citrus trees (unharmful to humans). Only pre-roasted Sichuan peppercorns are allowed, but they lose their numbing effect soon after roasting. This has not stopped the Chinese from giving up their love for those numbing-hot dishes. Stashes of genuine Sichuan peppercorns somehow find their way into Americans kitchens, to the delight of foodies and Sichuan transplants alike.

Water-boiled Beef
水煮牛肉

A most understated dish, the term "water-boiled" suggests nothing of the fiery cauldron that it actually is. Slices of beef are simmered in a red broth, seasoned with chili peppers, fermented chili-bean paste, soy sauce, and Sichuan peppercorns. The taste is numbing-hot, which not only clears sinuses but probably kills some bacteria as well. Upon serving, the rich beef stew is ladled over fresh lettuce or blanched Napa cabbage.

Mapo Tofu
麻婆豆腐

Meaning "Pockmark-face Lady's Tofu." During the War with Japan, a tofu-making lady in Chengdu sold this dish from a ramshackle street stand. Chengduers were immediately drawn to the aromas enhanced by the fried ground beef simmering in the wet-hot chili sauce. They talked about it by referring to the lady's poor facial complexion (mapo), which was marred with scars. The name stuck, and so did the dish's popularity. Adaptations of the recipe vary widely. It can even be found in Islamic and vegetarian restaurants.

"Fuqi Feipian"
夫妻肺片

Loosely translated as "husband-and-wife beef slices," this snack (just call it "feipian") was invented by a husband-and-wife team on the Chengdu streets. Master-cooked brisket and tripe are sliced and served cold with a drizzle of numbing-hot chili sauce and crushed peanuts. The red beef brisket is a good match with the white of tripe, and its tenderness is balanced by the tripe's chewiness. These contrasts symbolize the yin-and-yang of opposites, and complement the name of "husband-and-wife" with the meaning of a perfect union.

Wonton in Red Oil
紅油抄手

Wonton is popular all over China, but only in Sichuan are they daring enough to drape them in a red-hot chili sauce. Unlike the customary way of serving wontons in a soup, Sichuan wontons are eaten like

WESTERN

meat dumplings, coated with a distinctive wet-hot chili sauce without soup. The sauce itself is flavored with chili oil, soy sauce and peanut powder.

Dan-dan Noodles
擔擔麵

This is the quintessential street snack from Chengdu. It is a cold, meatless noodle, sold by vendors who walk around the city carrying an over-the-shoulder balance called "*dan.*" Thus, *dan-dan* is an affectionate term meaning, "noodles served from the dan." If you want a bowl of noodles, just flag a vendor down. The bowl of noodles is covered with a red-hot sesame sauce, and garnished with diced zhacai, chili oil, and peanut powder.

Ants Up a Tree
螞蟻上樹

Although the curious name suggests something exotic, this dish is no more than heaps of cellophane noodles stir-fried with ground pork. This dish is also bland – a slim minority in an otherwise fiery lineup of Sichuan specialties. Some people claim that this is actually a Hunan dish, although there is no concrete evidence suggesting that it is true.

Fish-flavor Eggplant
魚香茄子

Although the name suggests that this dish has something to do with fish, there is no fish in the fish-flavor. This is actually a vegetarian dish, and one of the interesting ways of preparing vegetables. The "fish-flavor" is the popular Sichuan technique for preparing fish – simmering it in a sauce of minced garlic, scallions and red chili. Sugar and vinegar provide the additional seasonings for a slightly tangy flavor.

Strange-flavor Chicken
怪味雞

Sichuan's "strange" flavor comes from a seemingly haphazard combination of five flavors: sweet, hot, sour, numbing, and saltiness. The result is another hallmark of Sichuan cookery: complex and unique; yet simple and understated. Cold pieces of boiled

AULD LANG ZHACAI

Remember the town scrooge that everyone loves to hate, until one day he is gone and everyone misses him? There is one such scrooge in Sichuan cuisine too – a humorless curmudgeon with an ear-splitting name: *zhacai*.

Zhacai is preserved mustard tubers – the underground portion of the mustard plant. Preserved in salt and red chili, zhacai must be washed or soaked in water before using in order to control its audacious punch. When purchased from the market, zhacai looks like a squat toad with blisters – not the most attractive item in the Chinese pantry. But the leathery exterior reveals a light and crunchy texture that does not break down even after prolonged cooking times. Thus zhacai is extremely versatile for added complexity in both flavor and texture, imparting a particularly rustic and spicy quality into the dish.

A classic recipe using zhacai is to stir-fry juliennes of it with pork. Diced zhacai can be used to flavor light soups. A bowl of fiery hot dan dan noodles is always garnished with a finely minced spoonful of zhacai sprinkled all over.

Fuling prefecture, near Chongqing, is the most famous area for zhacai production. The land is now submerged by the Three Gorges Dam project however. This has sent scientists scrambling to find new lands for the mustard crop – an effort that continues today. Fuling's purple soil rich in phosphorus and potassium may be nearly impossible to replicate, and no one has been fully satisfied with the "new" zhacai vying to take its place. A victim of progress and testimony to our tendency to overlook the mundane, old zhacai is now gone. Its memories will only last while our taste buds still remember, or until hopefully an equal or better zhacai is found.

chicken are topped with this sauce, allowing the strange flavors to soak through. It is excellent as an appetizer, and goes especially well with beer.

Twice-cooked Pork

回鍋肉

This is an interesting Sichuan dish in that it uses sweet bean paste – a northern Chinese condiment. Thin slices of pork belly are first boiled in water, and then fried. The frying part is crucial, because it creates a slight crispness in the fat. Fermented chili-bean paste provides a wet-hot flavor to the dish, and the sweet bean paste adds another dimension to this spicy dish.

Camphor-tea Smoked Duck

樟茶鴉

The Sichuan answer to the Beijing Duck is not quite the superstar as its northern cousin. The duck is marinated with star anise, black (Yunnan) tea, and orange peels. The smoking process uses more black tealeaves and camphor wood as the smoking base. The finished duck has a similar crispy-skin/tender-meat contrast like Beijing Duck. In Sichuan banquets, the camphor-tea smoked duck is almost universally served. It is not spicy at all, which is characteristic of all Chinese banquet dishes regardless of regional association.

Sichuan Hotpot ("Malaguo")

麻辣鍋

Sichuan has its own style of the Mongolian hotpot, which they call *malaguo*, or the "numbing-hot hotpot." The soup stock is covered with a layer of red chili oil. Beneath it is a fragrant broth containing star anise, chili peppers, and Sichuan peppercorns. When it starts boiling, the hotpot is something Harry Potter could well relate with.

YUNNAN DISHES

"Across the Bridge Rice Noodles"

過橋米線

Legend has it that the dish was invented by the wife of a Qing Dynasty official. When served in a restaurant, the dish comes to the table disassembled. One platter has the raw meat slices. Another platter has the rice noodles. And the bowl contains near-boiling chicken broth. The waitress first slides the thinly sliced chicken and pork into the broth. Rice noodles are added into the bowl next. All is completed with a garnish of cilantro, bean sprouts, and pea sprouts on top. The scalding broth quickly cooks the meats, and the lightly blanched vegetables round out a balanced, refreshing meal all in the same bowl.

Chicken in a Clay Airpot

氣鍋

The airpot is a cooking vessel unique to Yunnan. It is made of clay with a short chimney used for distributing steam inside the pot. The airpot is ideal for casserole types of dishes where foods are slowly simmered for hours. This dish features either a whole chicken or Cornish hen simmered with herbs and Chinese medicine. Very much a hearty chicken soup, this dish is capable of both warming souls on wintry days and cooling tempers in the dog days of summer.

Airpot (pinyin: qiguo)

WHERE TO EAT SICHUAN IN THE BAY AREA

Authentic Sichuan restaurants are rare; there may be two or three in the area that can claim this distinction. There are lots of "Szechwan" restaurants however, serving Guangdong cuisine with a splash of red chili. The food isn't necessarily bad. They just aren't the authentic Sichuan experience. As more mainlanders come, the situation is bound to change. As the most popular cuisine in China, Sichuan cuisine is quickly gaining new audiences in America. Chefs that once were afraid to offer *fuqi feipian* (or just "feipian"), water-boiled beef, and mapo tofu are starting to let fly all of their brazenness and heat. These and other dishes are now traveling on the fast track to stardom, soon to shatter the "Szechwan" stereotypes of yesteryear.

House of Sichuan
川蜀園

The authentic Sichuan stuff appears under the "Sichuan Special" and "Sichuan Style" sections of the menu. Several also appear on the hand-written board out front (although not all of them are). Skip the rest of the menu, which is a minefield of walnut shrimp, sweet-and-sour pork, and "Sichuan beef" designed to attract unsuspecting Americans. Assure the staff you want the real thing, so that you actually get the real thing.

20007 Stevens Creek Blvd., Cupertino
408.255.3328
11.30 – 21.30

Mastercard, Visa

South Legend Sichuan Restaurant
巴山蜀水

You won't find "Szechwan beef" here, but you will find some of the most authentic Sichuan stuff around. The fuqi feipian ("couple beef"), Chongqing-style chili-and-chicken, and water-boiled beef are all unabashedly dressed in bright red hues. Also try the Chengdu-style snacks on weekends: "Zhong's dumplings" in either chili oil or plain broth, dan-dan noodles, and hot-and-sour yam noodles (konnyaku). The predominantly Mandarin-speaking clientele and a far-end South Bay locale make this place a 180 from the tired old Chinatown experience of decades past.

1720 N. Milpitas Blvd., Milpitas
408.934.3970
11.00 – 21.00

Mastercard, Visa

Chinese Village Restaurant
川味軒

With a Sichuan chef and a Beijinger manager at the helm, you end up with a mixed menu of western and northern favorites. Sichuan dishes here do not let up with the heat. The fuqi feipian ("spicy combination" on the menu), "pon pon" chicken, and water boiled beef all come laden with enough chili to feed a Caribbean nation. Try the "west style spicy fish," which is made differently from the water boiling method.

1335 Solano Ave., Albany
510.525.2285
11.00 – 22.00

All credit cards

Sam Lok Restaurant
豆花飯莊

Authentic Sichuan cuisine in Chinatown?! Keep looking. The few representative Sichuan dishes are tamed down considerably for the neighborhood's clientele: tourists and generations-old Guangdong people. Consider this the introductory course to the spicy world of Sichuan, if you insist. But what you have here won't be anything like the Sichuan food found elsewhere around the Bay.

655 Jackson St., Chinatown
415.981.8988
11.00 – 22.00

Mastercard, Visa

Spices
辣妹子

Sichuan cooking has a different outlook in Taiwan, and it is reflected here at both Spices locations. Dishes are not as hot as those fired up by Sichuan natives, but here they have a fresher, less earthy taste by moving away from fermented condiments. The 6th Avenue location has more seafood and hybrid (pan-China) dishes. The 8th Avenue location serves more smaller-portioned snacks. Stinking tofu, for instance, is served deep-fried, in a hotpot, or as the basis of a putrid-smelling (that's the point) mapo tofu.

294 8th Ave., San Francisco (Richmond)
415.752.8884
11.00 – 21.45

Cash only

291 6th Ave., San Francisco (Richmond)
415.752.8885
11.00 – 21.45

Mastercard, Visa

Wentworth St., Chinatown

Shenjianbao

EASTERN CHINA

Eastern Chinese cuisine is commonly called "Jiangzhe" cuisine. For centuries, it was China's most sophisticated style of cooking. Many of China's most famous dishes come from this region. Characterized by rich, complex flavors and reliance on technique and skill, Jiangzhe cooking is by far the most difficult to master. Many consider it the apex of the Chinese culinary tradition.

A variation of Jiangzhe cuisine exists in Shanghai, the mainland's most cosmopolitan city. Up until 1949, Shanghai was the crossroads of foreigners and migrants from different parts of China. It also warehoused exotic ingredients from all over the world. In the decades leading up to communism, Shanghai's local cooking borrowed liberally from these available resources and transcended its Jiangzhe roots into something of a pan-China and fusion cuisine. Both Jiangzhe and Shanghai cuisines stagnated under communism, but as the Chinese economy booms, both are on for an amazing Renaissance.

Jiangzhe and Shanghai cuisines available in America today still barely scratch the surface of their deep-rooted heritages back home. Around town, the two cuisines are nearly indistinguishable, with nearly everyone serving *xiaolongbao*. However, it's just a matter of time before more of the region's specialties come to our shores, and names like "Dongbo pork," "jinhua ham," and "Wuxi spareribs" will be as much a part of our vocabulary as charsui pork, kungpao chicken, and Beijing duck.

JIANGZHE/SHANGHAI CUISINES

The Chinese refer to their eastern seaboard as "Jiangzhe," a term derived from the two provinces that dominate the region: *Jiang*su and *Zhe*jiang. The cooking is therefore called Jiangzhe cuisine. The region also contains two landlocked provinces further up the Yangtze – Anhui and Hubei, both of which have largely forgettable contributions to Jiangzhe's culinary traditions. Also a part of the Jiangzhe region is the self-administered municipality of Shanghai, which evolved with its own cuisine. This region, especially around the crossroads of the Yangtze and the Grand Canal, has always been China's most prosperous and sophisticated. Likewise, the region's cuisine is China's most lavish and creative. Up until 1949, it was China's haute cuisine.

Nicknamed the "Land of Fish and Rice," Jiangzhe benefits from the Yangtze and the East China Sea for a large variety of fresh and saltwater fish. The wealth of the region also allowed people to indulge in the best meats – especially the fattiest cuts of pork bellies and rumps. They are often braised or steamed to bring out their tastiest textures. The Jiangzhe palate is also finicky for fine ingredients, which were brought in by river, canal, or overland from China and abroad. As a result, the entire scope of Jiangzhe cuisine embraces multitudes of flavors and sensations.

Jiangzhe cuisine also has a reputation for being strikingly sweet and oily. In the past, peasants elsewhere could not afford to cook with sugar and fats, but Jiangzhe was wealthy enough to indulge in them. A popular cooking technique, called "red-cooking," uses rock sugar, star anise, and soy sauce to create a reddish caramelized glaze with a distinctive sweetness that typifies the common Jiangzhe dish.

SHANGHAI CUISINE

Shanghai was no more than a fishing village of 10,000 people back in 1800. By 1900, shortly 100 years later, it had become a city of millions, surpassing nearby Hangzhou as China's largest city. The tremendous growth was owed to foreign trade, which was forced upon China after the First Opium War. Shanghai's proximity to major trade routes made it the focal point of the country. The confluence of peoples created an international city like no other in China at the time. A new cuisine evolved as a consequence, emerging from the old Jiangzhe roots with considerable outside influences. Elements from sixteen regional styles can be found in its cooking, as well as western techniques and ingredients.

The *xiaolongbao* is one such Shanghai dish. It was originally a northern Chinese baozi, but in Shanghai they filled it with soup inside. It was peddled on the streets and popularity caught fire. Another exemplary dish, called "Squirrel-style" Boneless Fish, uses such western ingredients as ketchup and yellow onions for a completely cosmopolitan flavor. The ultimate association of these two dishes with Shanghai demonstrates the cuisine's tendency to embrace outside influences.

Jiangzhe and Shanghai cuisines today still reflect the types of cooking that was popular in China back in the 1930s. Decades of communist rule stifled much of their development after 1949, leaving these traditions in a time capsule. But as the region's prosperity surges ahead, changes will undoubtedly unleash new waves of creativity. For now, consider them as a glimpse to China's recent past, and perhaps a clue to what could have been to Chinese food if their progress were not interrupted by the tragedies in history.

EASTERN

Xiaolongbao

TYPICAL JIANGZHE DISHES

Jiangzhe dishes are generally opulent, and complicated in preparation. Unlike Guangdong cuisine, which uses stir-frying to achieve simple, natural textures, Jiangzhe cuisine resorts to techniques such as braising and "red-cooking" to achieve softer textures and full-bodied flavors. Jiangzhe cuisine also consumes a lot of pork – usually the better cuts such as pork bellies and rumps. These give Jiangzhe cuisine an unshakable reputation for being exceedingly oily.

Lion's Head
獅子頭

A Yangzhou specialty, Lion's Head is not dish of the endangered animal. Rather, it is a benign, oversized meatball made of pork. First deep-fried and then simmered in an earthenware hotpot, the reddish meatball resembles the mane of a lion. It is most often served as a hearty stew of Napa cabbage, tofu, and cellophane noodles. Lion's Head can also be red-cooked in a sweet sauce with green vegetables for more striking visual appeal.

Westlake Egg-drop Soup with Minced Beef
西湖牛肉湯

This starchy clear soup features minced beef and tofu cut into small cubes. Egg drop is added to thicken the soup, although in some versions, the eggs are dropped completely. In those cases, the soup is thickened with potato starch. In the Chinese dining custom, soup is served last as cleanser of the palate.

Dongbo Pork
東玻肉

Named after Su Dongbo, a famous Song Dynasty poet who was also an accomplished cook, Dongbo Pork demonstrates the cuisine's main characteristics: sweet, highly sophisticated, but rather oily. Pork belly is cut into a square piece, tied with string into a compact package, and then slowly simmered with soy sauce, rock candy, star anise, cinnamon bark, and Shaoxing rice wine. When completed, it glows red in color, and the meat remains tender to the easy pickings of the chopsticks. This is among the most difficult dishes to prepare in Chinese cuisine, and very few places in the U.S. offer it on the menu.

"Reduced-fat" Pork Belly (kourou)
走油扣肉

In the past, pork belly (bacon) is the meat of choice – prized for its tenderness and high fat content. In this tedious dish to prepare, an entire cut of pork belly is first parboiled, then marinated in soy sauce. It is then deep-fried followed by an immediate immersion into an ice bath. The meat is then sliced and steamed to allow all of the fats to drip away. The result is slices of pork belly (kourou) with an alluring balance between of crunchiness and tenderness in the fat. The "reduced fat" claim is spurious, however: the fat drippings are collected to be made into gravy.

Wuxi Spareribs
無錫排骨

It is a signature dish from Wuxi's popular boat cuisine. Red-cooked pork spareribs are slowly simmered in a dark, sweet sauce of ginger, soy sauce, star anise, and rock sugar, until the meat is tender and about to fall off the bones.

Sweet-and-sour Pork
糖醋排骨

The dish that became a takeout superstar had its origins in Jiangzhe, where the local sweet-and-sour sauce uses sugar and Zhenjiang black vinegar. The pork, cut into small bite-size pieces, is battered and fried until crispy, and then coated with this vinegar sauce. After the slow boat to America in the 19th century, the Guangdong immigrants replaced the sugar and vinegar combination with a tangy plum sauce.

Shredded Fish with Pine Nuts
松子魚米

Freshwater fish fillet is chopped to the texture of grains of rice, then quickly stir-fried with roasted pine nuts in a light broth. The fish is tender and the pine nuts are crunchy, and their contrasting colors and textures are the dish's main appeal.

EASTERN

Red-cooked Fish Tail
紅燒划水

The back half of the fish is its most tender part, and Jiangzhe cuisine makes good use of it – by red-cooking it. In the typical Jiangzhe fashion, soy sauce, Shaoxing rice wine, and Zhenjiang black vinegar are combined with rock sugar and star anise to create a sweet and tangy sauce. This cooking style often finds its way into Hongkong-style seafood houses, where it is often called the "Shanghai-style" sauce.

Fried Fish in Seaweed Batter
苔條黃魚

It's fish-and-chips without the chips but lots of character instead. Fish fillets are deep-fried in a flour batter with thin strands of seaweed inside. A salt-and-pepper dipping salt provides all the necessary accoutrements to enhance the flavors of this surprisingly simple dish. It originates from Ningbo, a city otherwise not known for good cooking. Reputed to season everything monotonically with salt, Ningbo did a good job in this case.

Shrimp stir-fried with Longjing Tealeaves
龍井蝦仁

This is a classic Jiangzhe dish, which uses freshwater shrimp of the Yangtze with longjing tealeaves from Zhejiang province. The sweetness of the shrimp is a good complement to the slightly smoky, nutty fragrances of the green tealeaves.

Braised Crab in Flour
麵拖蟹

Braising ingredients in flour is a cooking method originating from Ningbo. It is similar to the Guangdong style of "baking." Crab is cut up into pieces and lightly breaded with flour, deep-fried, and then braised in a broth. The starch in the flour naturally thickens the cooking broth into a savory sauce.

Braised Shanghai Cabbage in Crab Roe Sauce
蟹黄菜心

Shreds of crabmeat and golden clumps of crab roe are at the center of attention in this opulent vegetable dish. The blanched pieces of whole Shanghai cabbage – often arranged artistically on a large platter – sop up all of the delicate flavors of the starchy crab roe sauce.

Eel Stir-fried with Yellow Nira
韭黄鳝糊

This is a simple stir-fry of eels with yellow nira, both of which are typical ingredients of Jiangzhe cuisine. The flavorings are quite simple – just salt and a dash of soy sauce. Stir-frying is ideal for yellow nira, in order to maintain a certain degree of crunchiness and its sweet, slightly pungent flavor.

Vegetarian Yellow Sparrows
素黄雀

A *zhaicai* dish from the tradition of Buddhist monastery cooking (see chapter on Chinese Vegetarian Cuisine), the "yellow sparrows" are actually dumplings wrapped in flat sheets of tofu. The fillings consist of a chop suey of julienne bamboo shoots, salted greens, lima beans, and so on. The dumplings are sautéed and braised in a vegetable broth.

Yangzhou-style Fried Rice
扬州炒飯

To Americans, fried rice resembles off-brown mounds of flaky rice, dotted with frozen peas, carrots and bits of roast pork. Yangzhou-style fried rice is pale because it uses no soy sauce. Rice is stir-fried with eggs, chicken, ham, shrimp, mushroom, bamboo shoot, and peas. Sometimes, a starchy egg drop soup is poured over like a sauce. It is a lavish substitute for plain rice, or can be eaten as a simple meal in itself.

APPETIZERS

A typical Jiangzhe meal always starts with an appetizer. It is a sign of luxury that is routinely skimped over in other regions.

Drunken Chicken

醉雞

Boiled chicken is chilled, then soaked in a briny sauce made from rice wine and salt. Some restaurants use a special yellow rice wine called Shaoxing, brewed in the city in Zhejiang province of the same name.

Mock Duck
素鴨

Or sometimes called Vegetarian Duck, it is a dish with its origins traceable back to the Buddhist monasteries. Dried sheets of tofu are pressed tightly together to create a texture similar to duck meat. Spices and seasonings are added to make it taste like the real thing, and many of the well-made ones are quite convincing.

Five-spice Smoked Fish
五香燻魚

Freshwater carp is actually fried to a crisp, not smoked. Then it is allowed to dry, chilled, and marinated with a combination of fruit juices, vinegar, spices, and rock candy to give the fish a smoked flavor.

Crystal Xiaorou
水晶肴肉

Chopped pork is marinated in its own consommé, and then reconstituted like a terrine with a layer of pork skin on the bottom. Upon serving, xiaorou is cut into oblong rectangular blocks, and served with a dipping sauce of ginger and Zhenjiang black vinegar. Traditionally, the meat is cured with saltpeter (potassium nitrate, or pinying: xiao), which turns it bright red. But because saltpeter is also a carcinogen when consumed in large amounts, xiaorou these days are made with little or none of it.

Eight Treasures Meat Sauce
八寶辣醬

The combination of eight ingredients is a classic concept in Chinese cookery. In this example, the appetizer reveals the opulence of the Jiangzhe region. Any eight ingredients would work. Typical are diced dried tofu, bamboo shoots, mushrooms, lima beans, shrimp, peanuts, Jinhua ham, and chicken. They are stir-fried in sweet bean paste to create a savory meat sauce that goes well over plain rice or with just about anything else.

Drunken Crab
燴醉蟹

Not for the faint of heart, raw crab is marinated in a briny mixture of Shaoxing rice wine and salt. The slightly sweet alcohol content enhances the sweetness of the crabmeat. Raw crab has a gelatinous texture that appeal to many Chinese.

SWEET DISHES

Not really desserts, since the Chinese are proven dessert-lackeys. These few sweet dishes are all that Jiangzhe offers. Customarily eaten as snacks, they can also pass for desserts only because there is nothing else to satisfy the sweet tooth.

Eight Treasures Sweet Rice
八寶飯

"Eight treasures" is a popular theme in Chinese cooking. Already mentioned is an appetizer called Eight Treasures Meat Sauce. Similarly, a sweet rice pudding is made from eight ingredients that can include some of the following: glutinous rice, lotus seeds, red bean paste, plums, raisins, pineapple, mandarin oranges, and candied wintermelon. All are steamed together, traditionally with lard. Sometimes a sugar syrup flavored with osmanthus is poured on top upon serving.

EASTERN

Glutinous Rice Balls in Fermented Rice Wine Mash
酒釀湯圓

The fermented wine mash used in Jiangzhe cooking is white in color, unlike the earthier red variety from Fujian. It is light enough to be used as the basis of a sweet soup. Sometimes, glutinous rice balls are cooked together along with mandarin oranges and osmanthus flower petals.

TYPICAL DISHES OF SHANGHAI

Shanghai cuisine is a potpourri of styles from all over. Influences from the West and various parts of China can be readily detected. Mainly Jiangzhe in character, Shanghai dishes are more cosmopolitan.

Sometimes, it hard to tell a Jiangzhe and Shanghai restaurant apart, because their dishes often overlap. Look for the dishes below as indicator for Shanghai. Otherwise, single out one dish that many say is quintessentially Shanghai: the xiaolongbao.

Sweet-and-sour Fish, Squirrel-style
松鼠糖醋魚

"Squirrel-style" was the rage in the 1930s at Shanghai's Meiweizhai (美味齋), a popular restaurant that did not survive the communists. Preparation requires intricate knife work, in which bones are removed from the fish, and the resulting fillets resemble stripes of a squirrel. Chinese and western elements are blended together in this dish: the whole fish is red-cooked with sugar and vinegar (a Jiangzhe technique), and enhanced with the flavors of yellow onions, tomatoes, and ketchup (western ingredients).

Braised Sea Cucumbers with Shrimp Roe
蝦子烏參

This is one of the most famous Shanghai dishes. It first appeared in the 1930s at Dexingguan (德興館), another popular Shanghai place of the time. Slices of tender sea cucumber are red-cooked with sweet bean paste, a northern Chinese touch. Dried shrimp roe, red-orange in color, is added to enhance the appeal of the sauce.

Braised Fish Head

干燒魚頭

Jiangzhe dishes are heavier and fattier than Guangdong's. This is also the case with seafood. Braised fish head uses a sauce of sweet bean paste, soy sauce, Zhenjiang black vinegar, ketchup, and garlic. Though more complex, it is not necessarily better. Often it is the simplest technique that makes the best tasting seafood. Compare this with other seafood done in the Chaozhou and Hongkong styles.

Shrimp with Walnuts

核桃蝦

Tender whole shrimp is sautéed, then braised in a clear, starched broth. Crunchy, honey-glazed walnuts are sprinkled on the side. This dish later inspired an adaptation in Hongkong-style seafood, which uses mayonnaise and either walnuts or cashews.

Fish-flavor Scallops

魚香干貝

Shanghai's willingness to accept outside influences is on display with this Sichuan-inspired dish. The fish-flavor sauce uses garlic, scallions, and fermented chili bean paste. Generally used for cooking fish, it is proven versatile for anything from eggplant to pork, or in this case, to scallops.

Red-cooked Pork Rump using Rock Sugar

冰糖元蹄

One of Shanghai's most famous dishes is also one of the heaviest. An entire side of pork rump is slowly red-cooked in a brine of soy sauce, ginger, and rock sugar. The rump skin is the most prized part of the dish; it is first deep-fried so that it could absorb all of the cooking liquids. The skin and meat of the rump have an unbelievable tenderness that melts in the mouth. Typically, this dish is served over a bed of blanched spinach or Shanghai cabbage.

EASTERN

Red-cooked Bamboo Shoot and Mushroom
紅燒雙冬

The combination of bamboo shoots and mushrooms is what the Chinese call *shuangdong*, or "double winter." It comes from the notion that the best bamboo shoots and mushrooms are harvested during the winter. These days, the shuangdong theme can be found in all Chinese regional dishes, and at all times of the year.

Fried Wheat Gluten Stir-fried with Shuangdong
雙冬麵筋

Deep-fried wheat gluten (pinyin: kaofu) is an important ingredient in Chinese vegetarian cuisine, providing both a vital source of protein as well as meat-like textures that people naturally crave. It resembles a sponge in appearance, which can then be manipulated to look (and taste) like beef or mutton.

Stir-fried Rice Cake
上海炒年糕

A peculiar dish that is instantly identifiable as Shanghai is stir-fried rice cakes. Sliced pieces of whitish rice cakes made of glutinous rice stir-fried with different kinds of ingredients, just like fried rice. The consistency of the rice cakes becomes sticky and chewy. Popular Jiangzhe ingredients for stir-frying include yellow nira, kaofu, and pork bellies.

Xiaolongbao
小籠湯包子

The glories of northern dumpling-making skills are usurped by Shanghai as it own. The soupy baozi are so popular as street snacks that they can be found on nearly every Shanghai street corner. The pan-fried variation is called shenjianbao. It is the baozi equivalent of potstickers.

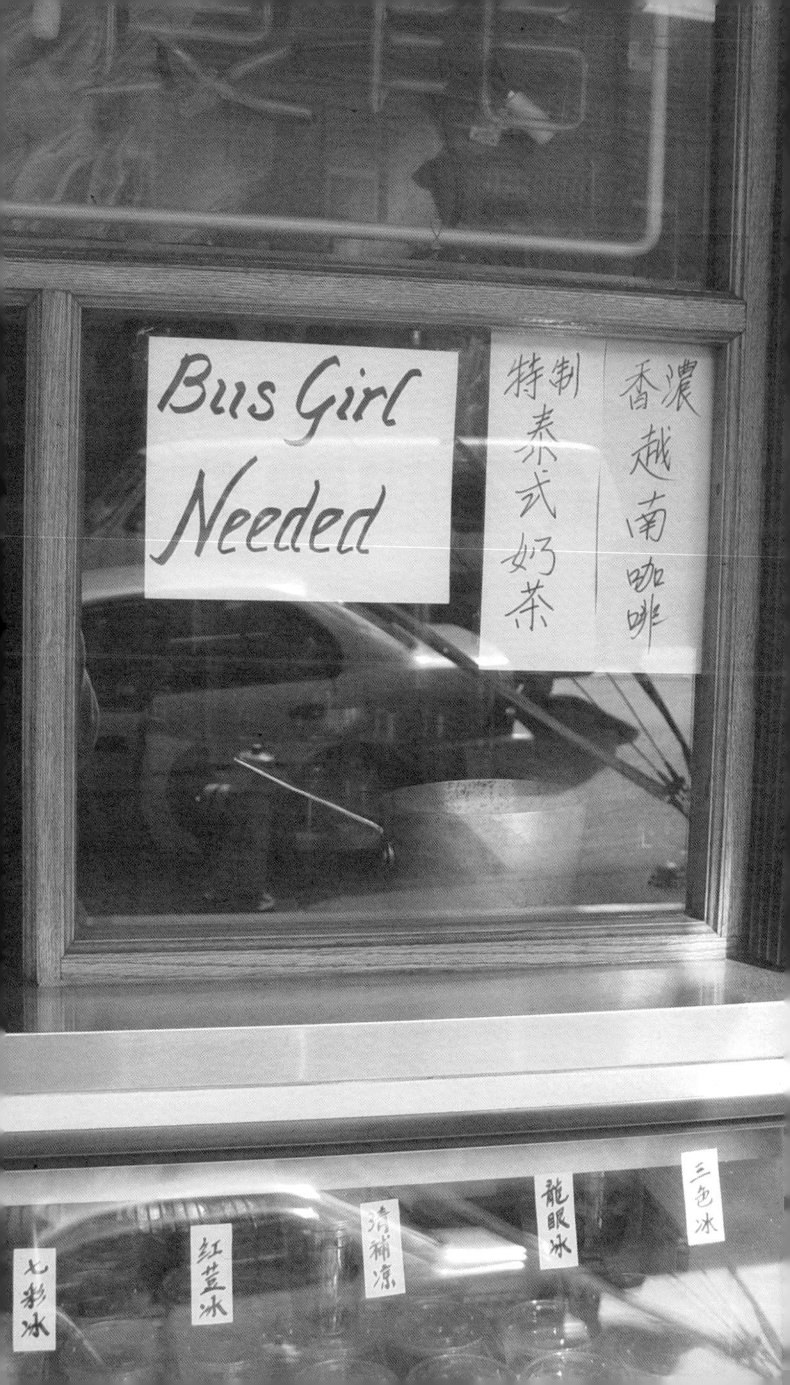
Bus Girl
Needed
特制泰式奶茶
濃香越南咖啡
七彩冰
紅荳冰
清補凉
龍眼冰
三色冰

WHERE TO EAT JIANGZHE/SHANGHAI IN THE BAY AREA

In recent years, Jiangzhe cuisine has become very popular. The richness of its cooking traditions is gradually redefining America's perception of Chinese food. That said, Jiangzhe is still a resurging trend, and the varieties available stateside are still slim pickings in comparison with what exists on the mainland.

Although Jiangzhe and Shanghai are separate cuisines, their distinctions in America are not so glaring. The main reason is that truly exemplary restaurants of either style are rare, and most restaurants tend to stick with a standard menu of classic dishes. For practical purposes, consider Jiangzhe cuisine as more traditional, while Shanghai incorporates more seafood and foreign ingredients. Also, Shanghai has the perennial favorite – xiaolongbao. But to blur the line even further, everyone is on the xiaolongbao bandwagon these days, even dim sum/yum cha houses.

Jiangzhe Cuisine

Taipei Stone House Seafood Restaurant
石家飯店

Stone (Shi) is the family name of the proprietors. The menu here embraces most of Jiangzhe's famous and classic dishes: shredded fish with pine nuts ("minced fish with 'endives'"), lion's head ("meat ball casserole"), crystal xiaorou ("jelly cold pork"), vegetarian yellow sparrows ("Buddha delight"), and fried fish in seaweed batter ("fish stick with seaweed"). Also ask if they have the more elaborate pork rump dishes on the daily menu.

10877 N. Wolfe Rd., Cupertino
408.255.8886
11.00 – 21.30

Mastercard, Visa

Won Stew House
萬家香滷味

The masters of master-cooking have set up shops in outer suburbia, where the Chinese congregate nowadays. You may find the varieties bewildering: beef brisket, tendons, duck, even pig's heart. These are meant to be taken away and served at home. Or you can get any of the above in a bento rice box to go. Other snacks like meat ball (wrapped in potato starch) and "tempura" (deep-fried fish cakes) reveal the place's Taiwanese lineage.

46813 Warm Springs Blvd., Fremont
510.683.0888
10.00 – 21.00

Mastercard, Visa

1715 Lundy Ave., #162, San Jose
408.392.9668
10.00 – 21.00

Mastercard, Visa

Jai Yun
佳園

Only dinner is served here, and there is no menu. The offerings are changed almost daily based on fluctuations in available ingredients. And the unassuming location provides center stage for sophisticated, banquet-style dishes. Jai Yun is quite an unusual restaurant, if not for the aforementioned facts, then because chef Nei's personality shows up in his dishes pure and through. Call ahead.

923 Pacific Ave., Chinatown
415.981.7438
19.00 – 21.30, closed Thursday

Cash only

Shanghai Cuisine

A & J Restaurant
半畝園

This Taipeier shop makes some mean Shanghai-style snacks, like pancakes stuffed with beef (and one with white radishes), xiaolongbao, and a flaky pastry called xiekehuang ("crab shell yellow"). Most of these are served only on weekends for breakfast, which you consume with soy milk. The rest of the day, the place offers simple noodles and small appetizers.

10893 N. Wolfe Rd., #C, Cupertino
408.873.8298
*11.00 - 21.00, at 08.00 on weekends
(for breakfast)*

1698 Hostetter Rd., #D, San Jose
408.441.8168
*11.00 – 21.00, at 08.00 on weekends
(for breakfast)*

Cash only

Ding Sheng Restaurant
上海鼎盛

Mainlanders may do things just a bit too authentic here: dishes are oilier than you may be used to. The reduced-fat pork rump ("braised pork in brown sauce"), lion's head ("braised meatball"), and braised fish tail are all expert examples of the region's famous red-cooking style. Shanghai-style street snacks like xiaolongbao, stir-fried rice cakes, and scallion pancakes are also available all day.

686 Barber Ln., Milpitas
408.943.8786
10.00 – 01.00

Mastercard, Visa

Star Lunch
上海小吃

A narrow grease-lined counter bisects this little diner. White walls and florescent lights provide all the necessary ambience. The stools on one side probably saw better days back when David Crosby still had hair. On the other side, the blackened stoves turn out a limited menu of rice and noodles on the fly. But the stinking tofu here is really tops. Home-made and the most foul-smelling around, it is only served on weekends (or in the late afternoon if you ask).

605 Jackson St., Chinatown
415.788.6709
11.00 - 18.30, closes at 15.00 on Mondays

Cash only

Vegetable market, Xinzhu prefecture, Taiwan

PAN-CHINA FOODS

Even though regional identities are particularly strong in Chinese food, there are a few things that are uniform throughout the country. These "pan-China" foods have no particular ties to any region, and they appeal to a broad audience suiting the varied palates of all Chinese.

Vegetarian cuisine is one such pan-China food. It evolved from Buddhist monasteries that served meatless dishes to monks and nuns. Travelers who sought shelter there eventually brought this cooking artform to the rest of the country. Not really a distinct cooking style, Chinese vegetarianism is more like an exhibition of Chinese ingenuity – a craft galvanized by religious faith and the love for food to become a very unique way of cooking (and eating).

Chinese bakeries on the other hand, are not an invention but the adaptation of western dessert-making traditions. Up until the 1800s the Chinese did not know how to bake with ovens, so these skills were borrowed completely from the Europeans. As time went by, Chinese bakeries began developing certain personalities of their own. Soon, Chinese breads and pastries began to look very "Chinese." Some of the trendiest bakeries today are so unusual that they are unlike anything the world can easily imagine.

CHINESE VEGETARIAN CUISINE

Is meat-eating such a hard habit to break? Many of us would be hard pressed to give up the omnivorous world that has, for better or worse, honed our taste buds for Spam and Kobe beef. But choosing a vegetarian lifestyle does not mean committing to a life of asceticism. The creative impulses of Chinese vegetarians have transformed the outlook of vegetarianism forever. What was once a realm of flavorless plants, extracts, and emulsions, vegetarian diet is made into a highly edible, even sophisticated, fare easily accessible to everyone.

First time visitors to a Chinese vegetarian restaurant may be struck by the menu. Where are the vegetable dishes? Beef, chicken, fish and pork are all unashamedly printed in bold *Times New Roman*. But these are not misprints or bad translations. The "meats" are so in name only. They remain vegetarian through the use of imitation meats. Often these imitations look so real they are hard to tell apart: "chicken" looks and tastes like chicken; "fish" fillets come in that familiar flaky texture, even with a dark, scale-less skin; and the "cuttlefish" has a similar crunchiness of the real thing. In the Chinese herbivorous world, vegetarians can have kung-pao chicken to their heart's content.

Chinese vegetarianism is not necessarily vegan. The Buddhist concept of *ahimsa* – meaning mercy and non-injury – teaches that people should avoid killing living things for food. In their view, eating milk, honey, and unfertilized eggs does not contradict this precept, so they are considered fair game to the ahimsa diet. Five types of vegetables are expressly *verboten* in the Buddhist diet: garlic, leek, nira, onions/scallions, and shallots. They are said to create bad odors, and contradictory to the ideal of spiritual cleanliness.

All varieties of non-animal ingredients are used: vegetables, fruits, fungi, algae, and legumes. The primary sources of protein come from soybean and wheat gluten. Tofu is pliable in all manners: used fresh, fermented, dried, pressed, rolled, stacked in sheets, et cetera. Red meats are often imitated with a wheat protein (gluten) called kaofu (Japanese: seitan). Another protein source called Textured Vegetable Protein, or TVP, is derived from soybean flour with all the oils extracted. It forms a sponge-like substance that resembles ground beef or pork.

THE DISHES OF CHINESE VEGETARIANISM

Since Chinese vegetarianism spans geographical boundaries, there is no regional specificity to vegetarian cooking. In fact, in the vegetarian restaurant you will find dishes from all over China represented on the menu. Just look for dishes that interest you. In many cases, the most rewarding experience is to sample your favorite regional dishes done with imitation meats.

The artistry of the imitation meats is the true personality of Chinese vegetarianism. Some look and taste so deceptively real that it is a wonder how much thought went into making these things. Tofu and soybean-based proteins make up the primary ingredient for the "meats." Kaofu and TVP appear frequently in dishes emulating red meats.

Mushrooms are also an important part of the vegetarian diet. Manipulated in different ways, they can substitute for poultry and various kinds of seafood. In other dishes, mushrooms are used fresh. Other fungi, such as white tree fungus and bamboo pith, are also regulars on the vegetarian table.

Chinese vegetarianism is a healthy lifestyle, but that doesn't necessarily translate into effective weight control. The dishes are *very* oily, because oil is used to bring out as much of the desired flavors and textures as possible. Vegetable oil is the de facto staple of Chinese vegetarianism. Otherwise, the glowing, rotund complexions of Buddhist monks and nuns wouldn't be so pronounced.

WHERE TO EAT VEGETARIAN IN THE BAY AREA

The proprietors of Chinese vegetarian restaurants are often strict vegetarians themselves, so the food is very much true to faith. Even though most Chinese are omnivores, many eat vegetarian on prayer days (days of the new- and full moons). Also, imitation meats are a touch of exotica that the Chinese also find fascinating, so a trip to these restaurants is an exciting experience for them as well.

Lu Lai Garden Vegetarian Cuisine
如來素菜館

Dishes here adhere to strict Buddhist orthodoxy: no garlic, onions, and the like (the "five pungents"). The stuffed eggplant, bell pepper, and tofu are vegetarian versions of the Hakka classic. They can be served in a black bean sauce or on a sizzling platter. Come here to explore how they imitate shrimp, octopus, and eel.

210 Barber Ct., Milpitas
408.526.9888
10.30 – 21.15

Cash only

Mother Nature Vegetarian Cuisine
大自然素食館

The "unchicken" and "unfish" are just their honest way of explaining these are really vegetarian dishes. But they look like the real thing, and taste like it too. There are also "kidney," "ham," and "shark fin" dishes on the menu. The beef satay can blow your mind.

843 San Pablo Ave., Albany
510.528.5388
11.30 – 21.00

Mastercard, Visa

Lucky Creation Vegetarian
如意齋素菜館

Not much imitation meats here, just honest vegetarian dishes featuring greens, tofu, and lots of mushrooms. The cooking style is Guangdong, so you can expect chow mein topped with kaofu (gluten), fried taro rice cakes, and earthenware hotpots.

854 Washington St., Chinatown

415.989.0818
11.00 - 21.30, closed Wednesday

Cash only

Bok Choy Garden
喜香園素食館

Another Guangdong-inspired vegetarian restaurant offers all sorts of beef, pork, chicken, and fish dishes. If you have time, stick around for the duck, shrimp, and cuttlefish. None of which is real meat.

1820 Clement St., San Francisco (Richmond)
415.387.8111
11.00 - 21.00, closed Monday

Mastercard, Visa

Hulu House Vegetarian Restaurant
葫蘆鄉素食小吃

Chinese-vegetarian meets Malay-Singaporean at this little junction. Dishes like laksa, nasi lemak, coconut rice with fish, and Hainan chicken rice are all things you find on the streets of Kuala Lumpur, but here they are sans meat, of course.

754 Kirkham St., San Francisco
415.682.0826
11.00 - 21.00, closed Tuesday

Mastercard, Visa

CHINESE BAKERIES

Dessert-making is the black hole of Chinese cookery. Besides just a handful of pastries that marginally pass for desserts, the Chinese do not have much of a legacy in these saccharin comestibles. Among the few sweets the Chinese make are mooncakes, longevity peach, and eight treasures rice. Most other pastries have foreign origins, coming mainly from Europeans over the past 200 years.

TRADITIONAL BAKERIES

The "classic" Chinese pastry is a thick, flaky medallion with fillings such as red beans, jujubes, lotus seeds, or ground sesame wrapped inside. Meats are often used as well. In essence, these pastries are baked dumplings, resembling baozi or jiaozi (see page 107).

These classic pastries are generally sold in traditional Chinese bakeries. In Guangdong, these bakeries make a variety of dim sum as well, such as shao mai and har gow. In nearly every traditional bakery, you will find the egg custard tart, which borrows from English and French influences to become a true Guangdong classic. The chicken roll, which is a cross between a chicken pot pie and an egg roll, is also nearly omnipresent.

MODERN CHINESE BAKERIES

Strictly traditional bakeries are slowly disappearing, especially in neighborhoods without a heavy concentration of the Guangdong people. The Chinese have gravitated toward cream-filled cakes more in-line with western tastes. Modern Chinese bakeries cater to this shift with a colorful phalanx of cakes and pastries much like the varieties found in

American bakeries. These bakeries churn out sponge cakes used in all forms of chocolate, tea, and nut-cakes. An occasional red bean pastry or a "taro surprise" lurks in the milieu, just in case you forget that these are actually *Chinese* bakeries.

Modern Chinese bakeries also make breads. The Chinese bread comes with a variety of fillings baked inside, just like what they do with dumplings. Scallion bread is the standard bakery fare. Other bread fillings run the gamut from hotdogs to cream of corn.

As for bread loaves, the Chinese have only one type that matters: it is a square-shaped white bread baked inside an enclosed rectangular box. There are no "top" and "sides" to this toast. Instead, the same leathery crust surrounds the entire loaf. The Chinese like to slice their toast much thicker than Americans. It is especially good for making French toast.

ZHONGZI-BINGING IN THE SPRING

Around mid-spring, traditional Chinese bakeries begin selling a green, fist-sized package called zhongzi. These are glutinous rice balls stuffed with a filling of some sort, and wrapped in bamboo leaves.

This is the food item for the yearly holiday of Duanwujie, which occurs on the fifth day of the fifth month of the lunar calendar. On the western calendar, it falls sometime between mid-May and mid-June. Although most people understand Duanwujie as a day of eating zhongzi and racing dragon boats, the real story behind it goes as follows:

Duanwujie is a tribute to the beloved poet Qu Yuan (340 - 278 B.C.), who lived during the tumultuous Warring States Period (476 - 221 B.C.) of the Eastern Zhou Dynasty. During this time, the Han dominion was divided into seven rivaling states (nations). A passionate patriot of the Chu state in the Lower Yangtze, Qu committed suicide by jumping into Miluojiang (a Yangtze tributary in northeastern Hunan) when he learned that Chu was conquered by the powerful Qin. The search party that went to recover him painted their boats with dragon faces to fend off evil spirits. They also dropped leaf-wrapped rice parcels into the river for him to eat, beating drums loudly to scare away the fish. Qu was never found, but the spirit of his search is remembered with the dragon boats, the beating drums, and the unabashed bouts of zhongzi-binging that have come to symbolize the modern face of the holiday.

The standard zhongzi filling is a mélange of pork, mushroom, and chestnuts. The glutinous rice is seasoned with five-spice. There are also sweet zhongzi of glutinous rice stuffed with either red bean paste or date paste. Trendy new flavors are also tested on the market every year.

Zhongzi can be either boiled or steamed. From the glutinous rice used, they have a very sticky consistency. In southern China there is an altogether different zhongzi "cured" with saltpeter. The chemical completely dissolves the rice during the cooking process, transforming it into a fillingless, translucent yellow-colored rice cake. This "saltpeter zhongzi" (pinyin: jianzhong) is served with a sweet syrup, or by sprinkling granulated sugar on top.

MOONCAKE-TRADING FOR THE FALL

If there is one traditional sweet that defines China, it must be the mooncake. The *Wall Street Journal* described them as "like Christmas fruitcakes in the U.S." Every year, when the waning days of August draws autumn to the fore, the Chinese fidget with a peculiar ritual of mooncake-giving.

Mooncakes were once treasured treats that people gladly ate up. Today, they are basically *comida non grata*. Receiving a box of mooncakes is like catching the flu: many quickly give it to a "friend" who then sends it on to someone else. There is an old joke that the original box of mooncakes is still being passed around somewhere.

Mooncakes are the central food item to the Mid-Autumn Festival, the Chinese equivalent of *Oktoberfest* packed into a single day of mooncake-stuffing festivities. The day occurs on the 15th day of the 8th month of the lunar calendar. It coincides with the full moon closest to the autumnal equinox, and also harvest time.

On this day, parents take their children out in the evening to view the full moon, and munch on mooncakes as they retell the legend of *Chang-e*. A mythical figure from antiquity, beautiful Chang-e drank too much of her husband's *Elixir of Life*, and was sent with her pet rabbit to exile on the moon.

Traditionally, mooncakes were made with a non-Atkins-compliant filling of mashed lotus seeds, lard, and sugar. Before, they were the once-in-a-year opportunity to indulgence in sebaceous sweets. Today, when food is plentiful, mooncakes have become passé. Despite updated versions that use vegetable oil instead of lard, or fancy ingredients like shark's fin, pineapples, and even *mochi*, mooncakes are headed the way of the bell-bottom and to the nadir of culinary infamy.

Many mooncakes have a salted duck egg yolk stuffed in the center. When such a mooncake is sliced in half, the bright orange yolk appears like a round moon. You can buy mooncakes either individually or in decorative gift boxes. Each dense, palm-sized mooncake weighs around two pounds. A prepackaged box usually contains four mooncakes, which are plenty to haunt an entire family for months.

WHERE TO FIND BAKERIES IN THE BAY AREA

There are so many Chinese bakeries around town, it is nearly impossible to account for them all. And few really stand out from the rest – they all typically offer similar selections of pastries, breads, and traditional dim sum. Here are a few traditional and modern bakeries that offer good and consistent quality.

Traditional Bakeries

Hong Kong Bakery
香港餅家

210 Castro St., Mountain View
650.578.0618

Sum Yee Bakery
新意糕點店

918 Webster St., Oakland
510.268.8089

Sun Sing Pastry
新城糕點店

382 8th St., Oakland
510.763.9228

ABC Bakery & Restaurant
ABC 餐廳餅家

650 Jackson St., Chinatown
415.981.0803

Cheung Yuen Dim Sum
昌源點心

648 Pacific Ave., Chinatown
415.834.1890

Louie's Dim Sum
新利園點心

1242 Stockton St., Chinatown
415.989.8380

Wing Sing
新永勝點心快餐

1125 Stockton St., Chinatown
415.433.5571

Modern Bakeries

Kee Wah Bakery
奇華餅家

1718 N. Milpitas Blvd., Milpitas
408.956.8999

386 Barber Ln., Milpitas
408.383.9288

Shun Kee
生記

10122 Brandley Dr., Cupertino
408.255.9999

10961 N. Wolfe Rd., Cupertino
408.865.1900

1842 N. Milpitas Blvd., Milpitas
408.262.3388

290 Barber Ct., Milpitas
408.428.9880

3288 Pierce St., Richmond
510.558.8807

1941 Irving St., San Francisco
415.753.1111

2964 S. Norfolk Blvd., San Mateo
650.341.8838

34332 Alvarado Niles Rd., Union City
510.477.9800

Sogo Bakery

10889 S. Blaney Ave., Cupertino
408.253.0388

46875 Warm Springs Blvd., Fremont
510.353.0988

471 Saratoga Ave., San Jose
408.554.0088

1610 S. De Anza Blvd., San Jose
408.861.0388

Barbecue shop, Oakland Chinatown

Appendix I: Restaurants by Area/City

SOUTH BAY/SILICON VALLEY

CUPERTINO

GUANGDONG

Joy Luck Place
醉香居
10911 N. Wolfe Rd.
Cupertino
408.255.6988
11.00 - 21.30
Mastercard, Visa

Silver Wing
銀翼飯店
10885 N. Wolfe Rd
Cupertino
408.873.7228
11.00 - 21.00
Mastercard, Visa

CHAOZHOU

TK Noodle
20735 Stevens Creek Blvd.
Cupertino
408.257.9888
09.00 - 21.00
Cash only

HOTPOT

Kingswood Teppan Steak House
上林鐵板燒餐廳
10935 N. Wolfe Rd.
Cupertino
408.255.5928
11.30 - 22.30, until 00.00 on
weekends
Mastercard, Visa

SICHUAN

House of Sichuan
川蜀園
20007 Stevens Creek Blvd.
Cupertino
408.255.3328
11.30 - 21.30
Mastercard, Visa

JIANGZHE

A & J Restaurant
半畝園
10893 N. Wolfe Rd., #C
Cupertino
408.873.8298
11.00 - 21.00, at 08.00 on
weekends (for breakfast)
Cash only

Porridge Place
旺旺清粥
10869 N. Wolfe Rd.
Cupertino
408.873.8999
11.30 - 23.00
Cash only

Taipei Stone House Seafood
Restaurant
石家飯店
10877 N. Wolfe Rd.
Cupertino
408.255.8886
11.00 - 21.30
Mastercard, Visa

BAKERY

Sheng Kee Bakery
生記
10961 N. Wolfe Rd.
Cupertino
408.865.1900

10122 Brandley Dr.
Cupertino
408.255.9999

Sogo Bakery
10889 S. Blaney Ave.
Cupertino
408.253.0388

TEASHOP

Ten Ren
天仁茗茶
10881 N. Wolfe Rd.
Cupertino
408.873.2038

MILPITAS

GUANGDONG

China First
中國第一
1741 N. Milpitas Blvd.
Milpitas
408.262.6226
11.00 - 21.30
Mastercard, Visa

Family Delight Café
家樂美食
662 Barber Ln.
Milpitas
408.943.8229
11.00 - 22.00
Cash only

New China Station B.B.Q.
Restaurant
新中國燒腊飯店
1828 N. Milpitas Blvd.
Milpitas
408.942.1686
10.30 - 21.30
Mastercard, Visa

New Hwong Kok
好旺角
1705 N. Milpitas Blvd.
Milpitas
408.263.8168
09.00 - 20.30
Cash only

Won Kee Seafood Restaurant
旺記海鮮酒家
206 Barber Ct.
Milpitas
408.955.9666
11.00 - 23.15
Mastercard, Visa

SEAFOOD

ABC Seafood Restaurant
富豪皇宮海鮮酒家
768 Barber Ln.
Milpitas
408.435.8888
17.00 - 21.30
All credit cards

Fu Lam Moon Seafood
Restaurant
富臨門海鮮酒家
1678 N. Milpitas Blvd.
Milpitas
408.942.1888
17.00 - 00.00
All credit cards

Kowloon Restaurant
海運大酒家
24 S. Abbott Ave.
Milpitas
408.945.8888
17.00 - 21.30
All credit cards

Mayflower Restaurant
五月花酒家
428 Barber Ln.
Milpitas
408.922.2700
17.00 - 21.30
All credit cards

DIM SUM/YUM CHA

ABC Seafood Restaurant
富豪皇宮海鮮酒家
768 Barber Ln.
Milpitas
408.435.8888
11.00 - 14.30, at 10.00 on
weekends
All credit cards

Fu Lam Moon Seafood
Restaurant
富臨門海鮮酒家
1678 N. Milpitas Blvd.
Milpitas
408.942.1888
11.00 - 14.30, at 10.00 on
weekends
All credit cards

Golden Island Chinese Cuisine
金島潮州酒家
282-286 Barber Ct.
Milpitas
408.383.9898
11.00 - 14.30, at 10.30 on
weekends
All credit cards

Kowloon Restaurant
海運大酒家
24 S. Abbott Ave.
Milpitas
408.945.8888
10.00 - 14.30
All credit cards

Mayflower Restaurant
五月花酒家
428 Barber Ln.
Milpitas
408.922.2700
11.00 - 14.30, at 10.00 on
weekends
All credit cards

Hongkong-style Coffeeshop
Café Ophelia-Milpitas
芳苑岩燒西餐
516 Barber Ln.
Milpitas
408.943.1020
11.30 - 22.00, until 00.00 on
weekends
Mastercard, Visa

Chez Mayflower
竹皇美食中心
416 Barber Ln.
Milpitas
408.894.9171
11.00 - 22.30, until 00.00 on
weekends
Cash only

Top Café
尖峰菜餐館
650 Barber Ln.
Milpitas
408.262.3338
11.00 - 03.00
Cash only

CHAOZHOU

Golden Island Chinese Cuisine
金島潮州酒家
282-286 Barber Ct.
Milpitas
408.383.9898
17.00 - 22.00
All credit cards

New Tung Kee
新潮州中記麵家
481 E. Calaveras Blvd.
Milpitas
408.263.8288
09.00 - 21.00
Cash only

Penang Garden
278 Barber Ln.
Milpitas
408.321.8388
11.00 - 22.00
All credit cards

TK Noodle
1792 N. Milpitas Blvd.
Milpitas
408.935.9888
08.00 - 20.00
Cash only

438 Barber Ln.
Milpitas
408.321.8889
09.00 - 21.00
Cash only

ISLAMIC-CHINESE

Darda Seafood Restaurant
清真一條龍
296 Barber Ct.
Milpitas
408.433.5199
11.00 - 21.30
Mastercard, Visa

DUMPLINGS & NOODLES

House of Noodles
老鄉麵館
690 Barber Ln.
Milpitas
408.321.8838
11.00 - 21.30
Cash only

HOTPOT

Café Ophelia-Milpitas
芳苑岩燒西餐
516 Barber Ln.
Milpitas
408.943.1020
11.30 - 22.00, until 00.00 on
weekends
Mastercard, Visa

Hot Pot City
可利亞火鍋城
500 Barber Ln.
Milpitas
408.428.0988
11.00 - 00.00, until 01.00 on
weekends
Mastercard, Visa

SICHUAN

South Legend Sichuan
Restaurant
巴山蜀水
1720 N. Milpitas Blvd.
Milpitas
408.934.3970
11.00 - 21.00
Mastercard, Visa

JIANGZHE

Shang Hai Restaurant
江浙聚豐園
1708 N. Milpitas Blvd.
Milpitas
408.263.1868
11.00 - 21.00
Mastercard, Visa

SHANGHAI

Ding Sheng Restaurant
上海鼎盛
686 Barber Ln.
Milpitas
408.943.8786
10.00 - 01.00
Mastercard, Visa

VEGETARIAN

Lu Lai Garden Vegetarian
Cuisine
如来素菜館
210 Barber Ct.
Milpitas
408.526.9888
10.30 - 21.15
Cash only

BAKERY

Kee Wah Bakery
奇華餅家
1718 N. Milpitas Blvd.
Milpitas
408.956.8999

Sheng Kee Bakery
生記
1842 N. Milpitas Blvd.
Milpitas
408.262.3388

Kee Wah Bakery
奇華餅家
386 Barber Ln.
Milpitas
408.383.9288

Sheng Kee Bakery
生記
290 Barber Ct.
Milpitas
408.428.9880

TEASHOP

Ten Ren
天仁茗茶
1732 N. Milpitas Blvd.
Milpitas
408.946.1118

SAN JOSE

GUANGDONG

Chef Ming
天天漁港
1628 Hostetter Rd., #F, G
San Jose
408.436.8868
09.30 - 21.30
Mastercard, Visa

Loon Wah Restaurant
龍華餐館
1146 S. De Anza Blvd.
San Jose
408.257.8877
11.00 - 21.30
Mastercard, Visa

New China Station B.B.Q.
Restaurant
新中國燒腊飯店
1710 Tully Rd., #A
San Jose
408.531.8008
10.30 - 21.30
Mastercard, Visa

HONGKONG-STYLE COFFEESHOP

Café 97
97 港式西餐
1701 Lundy Ave., #160
San Jose
408.573.8208
11.00 - 22.00
Cash only

Top Café
尖峰菜餐館
1075 S. De Anza Blvd.
San Jose
408.996.7797
11.00 - 03.00
Cash only

CHAOZHOU

Han Kee B.B.Q. Seafood
Restaurant
漢記潮州餐館
2017 Tully Rd.
San Jose
408.254.4665
08.00 - 22.00
Cash only

Kim Tar Restaurant
金塔粿條燒臘飯店
1698 Hostetter Rd., #J
San Jose
408.453.2006
10.30 - 00.00, at 09.30 on
weekends
Cash only

New Tung Kee
新潮州中記麵家
262 E. Santa Clara St.
San Jose
408.289.8688
09.00 - 21.00
Cash only

TK Noodle
1818 Tully Rd., #162B
San Jose
408.223.1688
08.00 - 20.00

261 E. William St.
San Jose
408.297.8888
08.00 - 20.00

336 N. Capitol Ave.
San Jose
408.937.1999
09.00 - 21.00

4068 Monterey Rd.
San Jose
408.365.1998
08.30 - 22.30

930 Story Rd.
408.298.1688
08.00 - 20.00

975 McLaughlin Ave.
San Jose
408.286.9000
09.00 - 21.00

All locations cash only

ISLAMIC-CHINESE

Fatima Seafood Restaurant
清真馬家海鮮館
1132 De Anza Blvd., #A
San Jose
408.257.3893
11.00 - 21.30
Mastercard, Visa

Ma's Restaurant
清真馬家館
1715 Lundy Ave., #168
San Jose
408.437.2499
11.00 - 21.30
Mastercard, Visa

JIANGZHE

A & J Restaurant
半畝園
1698 Hostetter Rd., #D
San Jose
408.441.8168
11.00 - 21.00, at 08.00 on
weekends (for breakfast)
Cash only

Won Stew House
萬家香滷味
1715 Lundy Ave., #162
San Jose
408.392.9668
10.00 - 21.00
Cash only

BAKERY

Sogo Bakery
1610 S. De Anza Blvd.
San Jose
408.861.0388

471 Saratoga Ave.
San Jose
408.554.0088

SANTA CLARA

CHAOZHOU

New Tung Kee
新潮州中記麵家
3577 El Camino Real
Santa Clara
408.261.8188
09.00 - 21.00
Cash only

EAST BAY

FREMONT

HONGKONG-STYLE COFFEESHOP

Café Ophelia-Fremont
芳苑咖啡西餐
46801 Warm Springs Blvd.
Fremont
510.668.0998
11.00 - 00.00
Mastercard, Visa

Finchi Café
海中天
46875 Warm Springs Blvd.
Fremont
510.657.1488
11.00 - 00.00, at 10.00 on
weekends
Mastercard, Visa

CHAOZHOU

New Tung Kee
新潮州中記麵家
39226 Argonaut Way
Fremont
510.795.2888
09.00 - 21.00
Cash only

HUNAN

Chili Garden Restaurant
火宮殿
3213 Walnut Ave.
Fremont
510.792.8945
11.30 - 21.30
Mastercard, Visa

HOTPOT

Café Ophelia-Fremont
芳苑咖啡西餐
46801 Warm Springs Blvd.
Fremont
510.668.0998
17.30 - 00.00
Mastercard, Visa

JIANGZHE

Shanghai Restaurant
三六九小館
46831 Warm Springs Blvd.
Fremont
510.668.0369
11.00 - 21.30, at 09.00 on
weekends
Mastercard, Visa

Won Stew House
萬家香滷味
46813 Warm Springs Blvd.
Fremont
510.683.0888
10.00 - 21.00
Mastercard, Visa

BAKERY

Mary's Bakery
美力斯精緻烘焙
34370 Fremont Blvd.
Fremont
510.796.7875

Sogo Bakery
46875 Warm Springs Blvd.
Fremont
510.353.0988

TEASHOP

101 Tea Plantation
101 茶園
46859 Warm Springs Blvd.
Fremont
510.623.9606

NEWARK

SEAFOOD

Royal Garden Seafood
Restaurant
豪景魚翅海鮮酒家
35219 Newark Blvd.
Newark
510.494.8989
17.30 - 21.30
Mastercard, Visa

DIM SUM/YUM CHA

Royal Garden Seafood
Restaurant
豪景魚翅海鮮酒家
35219 Newark Blvd.
Newark
510.494.8989
11.00 - 14.30, at 10.00 on
weekends
Mastercard, Visa

HONGKONG-STYLE COFFEESHOP

Cousin Café
表哥茶餐廳
39193 Cedar Blvd.
Newark
510.713.9806
08.00 - 23.00, until 01.00 on
weekends
Cash only

New Tung Kee
新潮州中記麵家
35201 Newark Blvd.
Newark
510.818.1136
09.00 - 21.00
Cash only

TK Noodle
39029 Cedar Blvd.
Newark
510.494.9200
09.00 - 21.00
Cash only

HOTPOT

Kingswood Teppan Steak House
上林鐵板燒餐廳
39055 Cedar Blvd.
Newark
11.30 - 22.30, until 00.00 on
weekends
Mastercard, Visa

Ninji's Mala Hot Pot Restaurant
寧記麻辣火鍋
6066 Mowry Ave.
Newark
510.792.2898
11.30 - 22.00
Mastercard, Visa

SICHUAN

Su Gia Restaurant
大四川
35233 Newark Blvd.
Newark
510.742.8777
11.00 - 21.30
Mastercard, Visa

JIANGZHE

King's Garden Chinese Cuisine
敘香小館
39055 Cedar Blvd., #189
Newark
510.792.5866
11.00 - 22.30
Mastercard, Visa

TEASHOP

Ten Ren
天仁茗茶
39115 Cedar Blvd.
Newark
510.713.9588

UNION CITY

SEAFOOD

China Villa Restaurant
馥林閣
34308 Alvarado Niles Rd.
Union City
510.475.8182
17.00 - 21.30
Mastercard, Visa

Lucky Palace Restaurant
新皇宮酒樓
34348 Alvarado Niles Rd.
Union City
510.489.8386
17.00 - 21.00
Mastercard, Visa

DIM SUM/YUM CHA

Lucky Palace Restaurant
新皇宮酒樓
34348 Alvarado Niles Rd.
Union City
510.489.8386
11.00 - 14.30, at 10.00 on
weekends
Mastercard, Visa

DUMPLINGS & NOODLES

Fortune Garden
一品香
1773 Decoto Rd.
Union City
510.487.9168
11.30 - 21.00, closed Tuesday
Cash only

SICHUAN

Szechwan Home
渝榕人家
34396 Alvarado Niles Rd.
Union City
510.324.5000
11.00 - 22.00
All credit cards

BAKERY

Sheng Kee Bakery
生記
34332 Alvarado Niles Rd.
Union City
510.477.9800

DALY CITY

SEAFOOD

Koi Palace
鯉魚門海鮮茶寮
365 Gellert Blvd.
Daly City
650.992.9000
17.00 - 21.30
All credit cards

DIM SUM/YUM CHA

Koi Palace
鯉魚門海鮮茶寮
365 Gellert Blvd.
Daly City
650.992.9000
11.00 - 14.30, at 10.00 on
weekends
All credit cards

CHAOZHOU

TK Noodle
6917 Mission St.
Daly City
650.994.8886
10.00 - 22.00
Cash only

HOTPOT

Koi Palace
鯉魚門海鮮茶寮
365 Gellert Blvd.
Daly City
650.992.9000
17.00 - 21.30
All credit cards

MILLBRAE

GUANGDONG

Chueung Hing Restaurant
祥興燒臘小館
241-245 El Camino Real
Millbrae
650.652.3938
10.30 - 21.30
Mastercard, Visa

SEAFOOD

Fook Yuen Seafood Restaurant
馥苑海鮮酒家
195 El Camino Real
Millbrae
650.692.8600
17.30 - 21.30
All credit cards

Hong Kong Flower Lounge
香港香滿樓
51 Millbrae Ave.
Millbrae
650.692.6666
17.00 - 21.30
All credit cards

DIM SUM/YUM CHA

Fook Yuen Seafood Restaurant
馥苑海鮮酒家
195 El Camino Real
Millbrae
650.692.8600
11.00 - 14.30, at 10.00 on
weekends
All credit cards

Hong Kong Flower Lounge
香港香滿樓
51 Millbrae Ave.
Millbrae
650.692.6666
11.00 - 14.30, at 10.30 on
weekends
All credit cards

MOUNTAIN VIEW

GUANGDONG

Café Yulong
玉龍小館
743 W. Dana St.
Mountain View
650.960.1677
11.30 - 21.30, until 22.30 on
weekends
All credit cards

Fu Lam Mum Seafood
Restaurant
富臨門海鮮酒家
246 Castro St.
Mountain View
650.967.1689
11.00 - 00.00
All credit cards

Hangen Szechwan Restaurant
漢金
134 Castro St.
Mountain View
650.964.8881
11.00 - 21.30
Mastercard, Visa

Man Bo Duck Restaurant
萬寶鴨子樓
360 Castro St.
Mountain View
650.961.6635
11.00 - 00.00, until 01.00 on
weekends
All credit cards

CHAOZHOU

New Tung Kee
新潮州中記麵家
520 Showers Dr.
Mountain View
650.947.8888
09.00 - 21.00
Cash only

TK Noodle
357 Castro St.
Mountain View
650.605.1200
09.00 - 21.00
Cash only

HUNAN

Hunan Chili
香辣軒
102 Castro St.
Mountain View
650.969.8968
11.00 - 21.30
All credit cards

DUMPLINGS & NOODLES

Café Yulong
玉龍小館
743 W. Dana St.
Mountain View
650.960.1677
11.30 - 21.30, until 22.30 on
weekends
All credit cards

VEGETARIAN

Garden Fresh Vegetarian
Restaurant
香根菜
1245 W. El Camino Real
Mountain View
650.961.7795
11.00 - 21.30, until 22.00 on
weekends
Mastercard, Visa

BAKERY

Hong Kong Bakery
香港餅家
210 Castro St.
Mountain View
650.578.0618

PALO ALTO

GUANGDONG

Peking Duck Restaurant
鴨子閣
2310 El Camino Real
Palo Alto
650.856.3338
11.00 - 21.30
All credit cards

SAN BRUNO

JIANGZHE

Shanghai Town Restaurant
小江南
189 El Camino Real
San Bruno
650.615.9879
11.00 - 21.30
Mastercard, Visa

SAN MATEO

HAKKA

Hakka Restaurant
客人之家
137 E. 3rd Ave.
San Mateo
650.348.3559
11.00 - 21.00
Mastercard, Visa

ISLAMIC-CHINESE

Fatima Seafood Restaurant
清真馬家海鮮館
1208 S. El Camino Real
San Mateo
650.554.1818
11.00 - 21.30
Mastercard, Visa

DUMPLINGS & NOODLES

Sun Tung Restaurant
山東小館
153 S. B St.
San Mateo
650.342.5330
11.30 - 21.00, at 10.30 on
weekends. Closed Monday
Mastercard, Visa

BAKERY

Sheng Kee Bakery
生記
2964 S. Norfolk Blvd.
San Mateo
650.341.8838

SAN FRANCISCO

GUANGDONG

CHINATOWN

ABC Bakery & Restaurant
ABC 餐廳餅家
650 Jackson St.
Chinatown
415.981.0803

Chef Jia's
喜福家
925 Kearny St.
Chinatown
415.398.1626
11.30 - 22.00
Cash only

Chung King Restaurant
江南海鮮店
606 Jackson St.
Chinatown
415.986.3899
11.30 - 21.30
Mastercard, Visa

DPD Restaurant
中山小館
901 Kearny St.
Chinatown
415.398.4598
11.00 - 00.00, at 15.00 on Sunday
Cash only

Hon's Wun-Tun House (CA.)
Ltd.
洪記麵家
648 Kearny St.
Chinatown
415.433.3966
11.00 - 19.00, closed Sunday
Cash only

Little Garden Seafood Restaurant
新龍樓
750 Vallejo St.
Chinatown
415.788.2328
11.00 - 21.30
Mastercard, Visa

Louie's California Chinese
Cuisine
鑫源酒家
646 Washington St.
Chinatown
415.291.8038
17.00 - 22.00
All credit cards

Po Kee Restaurant
寶記粥麵飯店
1365 Stockton St.
Chinatown
415.788.7071
10.00 - 21.30
Cash only

R&G Lounge
嶺南小館
631 Kearny St.
Chinatown
415.982.7877
11.00 - 21.30
All credit cards

Silver Restaurant
銀輝燒臘海鮮
737 Washington St.
Chinatown
415.434.4998
11.00 - 00.00
All credit cards

Young's Café
寶馬餐廳
601 Kearny St.
Chinatown
415.397.3455
10.00 - 21.00, closed Sundays
All credit cards

RICHMOND DISTRICT

ABC Bakery & Restaurant
ABC 餐廳餅家
2500 Noriega St.
San Francisco (Richmond)
415.681.8800
07.00 - 03.00
Cash only

Family Fortune Restaurant
鑫培旺
5037 Geary Blvd.
San Francisco (Richmond)
415.221.8831
11.00 - 22.00
All credit cards

Kam's Restaurant
金華餐館
3620-24 Balboa St.
San Francisco (Richmond)
415.752.6355
11.00 - 21.00
All credit cards

Sun Wu Kong Restaurant
新滬江大飯店
5423 Geary Blvd.
San Francisco (Richmond)
415.876.2828
11.00 - 22.00

Tai San Restaurant
鴻圖小館
3420 Balboa St.
San Francisco (Richmond)
415.752.3362
11.00 - 21.30, closed Mondays
Cash only

SEAFOOD

CHINATOWN

Chinatown Restaurant
新杏香酒樓
8 Wentworth Alley
Chinatown
415.392.7958
10.00 - 22.00
All credit cards

Great Eastern Restaurant
泩賓閣
649 Jackson St.
Chinatown
415.986.2500
15.30 - 01.00
All credit cards

New Asia Chinese Restaurant
新亞洲大酒樓
772 Pacific Ave.
Chinatown
415.391.6666
17.00 - 21.00
Mastercard, Visa

Pearl City Seafood Restaurant
新珠城海鮮酒樓
641 Jackson St.
Chinatown
415.398.8383
15.00 - 22.00, until 23.00 on weekends
Mastercard, Visa

Y. Ben House
會賓樓
835 Pacific Ave.
Chinatown
415.397.3168
16.00 - 21.00
Mastercard, Visa

RICHMOND DISTRICT
Lucky Fortune Seafood Restaurant
新福滿樓海鮮酒樓
5715 Geary Blvd.
San Francisco (Richmond)
415.751.2888
15.00 - 23.00
Mastercard, Visa

Mayflower Restaurant
五月花酒家
6255 Geary Blvd.
San Francisco (Richmond)
415.387.8338
17.00 - 21.30
All credit cards

ELSEWHERE
Harbor Village Restaurant
海景假日翠亨沌茶寮
4 Embarcadero Center, Lobby Level
San Francisco
415.781.7833
17.30 - 21.30
All credit cards

DIM SUM/YUM CHA

CHINATOWN
Chinatown Restaurant
新杏香酒樓
8 Wentworth Alley
Chinatown
415.392.7958
10.00 - 15.00
All credit cards

Great Eastern Restaurant
迓賓閣
649 Jackson St.
Chinatown
415.986.2500
10.00 - 15.00
All credit cards

Louie's California Chinese Cuisine
鑫源酒家
646 Washington St.
Chinatown
415.291.8038
10.00 - 15.00
All credit cards

New Asia Chinese Restaurant
新亞洲大酒樓
772 Pacific Ave.
Chinatown
415.391.6666
09.00 - 15.00
Mastercard, Visa

Pearl City Seafood Restaurant
新珠城海鮮酒樓
641 Jackson St.
Chinatown
415.398.8383
08.00 - 15.00
Mastercard, Visa

Y. Ben House
會賓樓
835 Pacific Ave.
Chinatown
415.397.3168
07.00 - 15.00
Mastercard, Visa

RICHMOND DISTRICT
Lucky Fortune Seafood Restaurant
新福滿樓海鮮酒樓
5715 Geary Blvd.
San Francisco (Richmond)
415.751.2888
10.00 - 15.00
Mastercard, Visa

Ton Kiang
東江
5821 Geary Blvd.
San Francisco (Richmond)
415.387.8273
10.30 - 22.00
All credit cards

Mayflower Restaurant
五月花酒家
6255 Geary Blvd.
San Francisco (Richmond)
415.387.8338
11.00 - 14.30
All credit cards

ELSEWHERE
Harbor Village Restaurant
海景假日翠亨沌茶寮
4 Embarcadero Center, Lobby Level
San Francisco
415.781.7833
11.00 - 14.30, at 10.30 on weekends
All credit cards

Yank Sing
羊城茶室
101 Spear St. (One Rincon Center)
San Francisco
415.957.9300
11.00 - 15.00 weekdays, 10.00 - 16.00 weekends
All credit cards

49 Stevenson St.
San Francisco
415.541.4949
11.00 - 15.00
All credit cards

HONGKONG-STYLE COFFEESHOP

New Hollywood Bakery & Restaurant
荷里活茶餐廳
652 Pacific Ave.
Chinatown
415.397.9919
07.00 - 18.00
Cash only

Sterling Ruby Restaurant
紅寶石餐廳
640 Jackson St.
Chinatown
415.982.0618
07.30 - 21.30
Mastercard, Visa

Washington Bakery & Restaurant
華盛頓茶餐廳
733 Washington St.
Chinatown
415.397.3232
07.30 - 21.00
Mastercard, Visa

CHAOZHOU

Capitol Kim Tar Restaurant
金塔粿條麵
758 Pacific Ave.
Chinatown
415.956.8533
09.00 - 21.00
Cash only

HUNAN

Brandy Ho's Hunan Food
何家湖南
217 Columbus Ave.
Chinatown
415.788.7527
11.00 - 23.30
All credit cards

Hunan Home's Restaurant
湖南又一村
622 Jackson St.
Chinatown
415.982.2844
11.30 - 21.30
All credit cards

HAKKA

CHINATOWN
Mon Kiang Restaurant
梅江飯店
683 Broadway St.
Chinatown
415.421.2015
11.00 - 22.00
Mastercard, Visa

RICHMOND DISTRICT
Dragon River Restaurant
龍江飯店
5045 Geary Blvd.
San Francisco (Richmond)
415.387.8512
11.00 - 21.30
Mastercard, Visa

Ton Kiang
東江
5821 Geary Blvd.
San Francisco (Richmond)
415.387.8273
10.30 - 22.00
All credit cards

ISLAMIC-CHINESE

SUNSET DISTRICT
Old Mandarin Islamic Restaurant
老北京
3132 Vincente St.
San Francisco (Sunset)
415.564.3481
11.30 - 21.30, at 17.30 on
Tuesdays
Mastercard, Visa

DUMPLINGS & NOODLES

The Pot Sticker
焗京
150 Waverly Pl.
Chinatown
415.397.9985
11.00 - 22.00
Mastercard, Visa

HOTPOT

Old Mandarin Islamic Restaurant
老北京
3132 Vincente St.
San Francisco (Sunset)
415.564.3481
11.30 - 21.30, at 17.30 on
Tuesdays
Mastercard, Visa

SICHUAN

CHINATOWN
Sam Lok Restaurant
豆花飯莊
655 Jackson St.
Chinatown
415.981.8988
11.00 - 22.00
Mastercard, Visa

RICHMOND DISTRICT
Spices
辣妹子
291 6th Ave.
San Francisco (Richmond)
415.752.8885
11.00 - 21.45
Mastercard, Visa

294 8th Ave.
San Francisco (Richmond)
415.752.8884
11.00 - 21.45
Cash only

JIANGZHE

Jai Yun
佳園
923 Pacific Ave.
Chinatown
415.981.7438
19.00 - 21.30, closed Thursday
Cash only

SHANGHAI

CHINATOWN
Star Lunch
上海小吃
605 Jackson St.
Chinatown
415.788.6709
11.00 - 18.30, closes at 15.00
Mondays
Cash only

RICHMOND DISTRICT
Shanghai Dumpling Shop
上海飽餃店
3319 Balboa St.
San Francisco (Richmond)
415.387.2088
11.00 - 21.00, opens 10.00 on
weekends
Cash only

VEGETARIAN

CHINATOWN
Lucky Creation Vegetarian
如意齋素菜館
854 Washington St.
Chinatown
415.989.0818
11.00 - 21.30, closed Wednesday
Cash only

RICHMOND DISTRICT
Bok Choy Garden
喜香園素食館
1820 Clement St.
San Francisco (Richmond)
415.387.8111
11.00 - 21.00, closed Monday
Mastercard, Visa

ELSEWHERE
Golden Era Vegetarian
Restaurant
572 O'Farrell St.
San Francisco
415.673.3136
11.00 - 21.00, closed Tuesday
Mastercard, Visa

Hulu House Vegetarian
Restaurant
葫蘆鄉素食小吃
754 Kirkham St.
San Francisco
415.682.0826
11.00 - 21.00, closed Tuesday
Mastercard, Visa

Shangri-La Chinese Vegetarian
Restaurant
香格裡拉
2026 Irving St.
San Francisco
415.731.2548
11.30 - 21.00
Mastercard, Visa

BAKERY

CHINATOWN
ABC Bakery & Restaurant
ABC 餐廳餅家
650 Jackson St.
Chinatown
415.981.0803

Cheung Yuen Dim Sum
昌源點心
648 Pacific Ave.
Chinatown
415.834.1890

Louie's Dim Sum
新利園點心
1242 Stockton St.
Chinatown
415.989.8380

Washington Bakery & Restaurant
華盛頓茶餐廳
733 Washington St.
Chinatown
415.397.3232

Wing Sing
新永勝點心快餐
1125 Stockton St.
Chinatown
415.433.5571

ELSEWHERE
Sheng Kee Bakery
生記
1941 Irving St.
San Francisco
415.753.1111

TEASHOP

Imperial Tea Court
裕隆茶莊
1411 Powell St.
Chinatown
415.788.6080
11.00 - 18.30, closed Tuesdays
All credit cards

Ferry Bldg.
San Francisco
415.544.9830
10.00 - 18.00, closed Mondays
All credit cards

Ten Ren
天仁茗茶
949 Grant Ave.
Chinatown
415.362.0656

OAKLAND/CONTRA COSTA

ALBANY

DUMPLINGS & NOODLES

Chinese Village Restaurant
川味軒
1335 Solano Ave.
Albany
510.525.2285
11.00 - 22.00
All credit cards

HOTPOT

Chinese Village Restaurant
川味軒
1335 Solano Ave.
Albany
510.525.2285
11.00 - 22.00
All credit cards

SICHUAN

Chinese Village Restaurant
川味軒
1335 Solano Ave.
Albany
510.525.2285
11.00 - 22.00
All credit cards

VEGETARIAN

Mother Nature Vegetarian
Cuisine
大自然素食館
843 San Pablo Ave.
Albany
510.528.5388
11.30 - 21.00
Mastercard, Visa

OAKLAND

GUANGDONG

Chef Lau's
佛笑樓海鮮館
301 8th St.
Oakland
510.835.3288
11.00 - 21.30, dinner only on
Tuesdays
All credit cards

Fortune Restaurant
福臨門酒家
940 Webster St.
Oakland
510.839.9697
11.00 - 02.30
Mastercard, Visa

Gold Medal Restaurant
金牌燒臘店
381 8th St.   Oakland
510.268.8484
09.00 - 21.00
Cash only

Gum Wah Restaurant
金華燒臘麵家
345 8th St.
Oakland
510.834.3103
08.00 - 19.00
Cash only

Happy Families Restaurant
天喜海鮮酒家
304 10th St.
Oakland
510.839.8871
09.00 - 21.30
Mastercard, Visa

Joy Luck Restaurant
敘樂酒家
327 8th St.
Oakland
510.832.4270
08.30 - 21.30
Mastercard, Visa

King Wah Restaurant
瓊華酒家
383 9th St.
Oakland
510.834.9769
11.00 - 21.00
Cash only

New Oakland Seafood
Restaurant
天倫海鮮酒家
307 10th St.
Oakland
510.893.3388
11.30 - 00.00
Mastercard, Visa

Sun Hing Meat Market
新興燒臘
386 8th St.
Oakland
510.836.1819
09.00 - 18.30
Cash only

Sun Hong Kong Restaurant
新香港酒家
389 8th St.
Oakland
510.465.1940
09.00 - 03.00
Cash only

Tin's Tea House Restaurant
醉瓊樓
701 Webster St.
Oakland
510.832.7661
09.00 - 21.30
All credit cards

Ying Kee Noodle House
英記麵家
373 8th St.
Oakland
510.251.1238
09.30 - 21.30
Cash only

Ying Kee Restaurant
英記食家
387 9th St.
Oakland
510.465.1888
09.30 - 21.30
Cash only

Yo Ho Restaurant
永和美食
337 8th St.
Oakland
510.268.0233
05.00 - 21.30
Mastercard, Visa

Yung Kee Restaurant
鏞記
888 Webster St.
Oakland
510.839.2010
09.00 - 02.00, until 03.00 on
weekends
Cash only

SEAFOOD

Restaurant Peony
牡丹閣海鮮酒家
388 9th St., #288
Oakland
510.286.8866
17.30 - 21.30
All credit cards

Jade Villa
翠苑
800 Broadway
Oakland
510.839.1688
09.30 - 21.00
Mastercard, Visa

Legendary Palace
燕喜樓
708 Franklin St.
Oakland
510.663.9188
17.00 - 23.00
Mastercard, Visa

Silver Dragon
銀龍酒家
835 Webster St.
Oakland
510.893.3748
11.30 - 20.30
All credit cards

DIM SUM/YUM CHA

Restaurant Peony
牡丹閣海鮮酒家
388 9th St., #288
Oakland
510.286.8866
11.00 - 15.00, at 10.00 on
weekends
All credit cards

Jade Villa
翠苑
800 Broadway
Oakland
510.839.1688
09.30 - 14.30
Mastercard, Visa

Joy Luck Restaurant
敘樂酒家
327 8th St.
Oakland
510.832.4270
08.30 - 14.30
Mastercard, Visa

Legendary Palace
燕喜樓
708 Franklin St.
Oakland
510.663.9188
10.00 - 14.30, at 09.00 on
weekends
Mastercard, Visa

Yo Ho Restaurant
永和美食
337 8th St.
Oakland
510.268.0233
09.00 - 14.30
Mastercard, Visa

HONGKONG-STYLE COFFEESHOP

D&A Café
文記茶餐廳
702 Webster St.
Oakland
510.839.6223
08.00 - 19.00
Cash only

CHAOZHOU

Vien Huong Restaurant
遠香菇室
712 Franklin St.
Oakland
510.465.5938
07.30 - 19.00
Cash only

DUMPLINGS & NOODLES

Shan Dong Mandarin Restaurant
山東館
328 10th St.
Oakland
510.839.2299
10.00 - 21.30
All credit cards

SHANGHAI

Shanghai Restaurant
上海小吃
930 Webster St.
Oakland
510.465.6878
11.00 - 22.00, until 01.00 on
weekends, lunch only Tuesdays
Mastercard, Visa

BAKERY

ABC Bakery & Restaurant
ABC 餐廳餅家
388 9th St., #186
Oakland
510.836.2288

Sum Yee Bakery
新意糕點店
918 Webster St.
Oakland
510.268.8089

Sun Sing Pastry
新城糕點店
382 8th St.
Oakland
510.763.9228

Tao Yuen Pastry
桃園糕粉店
816 Franklin St.
Oakland
510.834.9200

RICHMOND

GUANGDONG

Daimo Chinese Restaurant
地茂館香港美食
3288-A Pierce St.
Richmond
510.527.3888
09.00 - 03.00
Mastercard, Visa

SEAFOOD

Pacific East Seafood Restaurant
東太海鮮酒樓
3288 Pierce St., #A118
Richmond
510.527.8968
11.00 - 03.00 until 04.00 on
weekends
Mastercard, Visa

Saigon Seafood Harbor
Restaurant
西貢漁港
3150 Pierce St.
Richmond
510.559.9388
11.00 - 23.00
Mastercard, Visa

DIM SUM/YUM CHA

Pacific East Seafood Restaurant
東太海鮮酒樓
3288 Pierce St., #A118
Richmond
510.527.8968
11.00 - 15.00, until 16.00 on
weekends
Mastercard, Visa

Saigon Seafood Harbor
Restaurant
西貢漁港
3150 Pierce St.
Richmond
510.559.9388
11.00 - 15.00
Mastercard, Visa

HONGKONG-STYLE COFFEESHOP

Orchid Bowl Café
澳門街
3288 Pierce St., #C156
Richmond
510.559.7888
11.00 - 22.00
Mastercard, Visa

CHAOZHOU

VH Noodle House
遠香
3288 Pierce St., #B101
Richmond
510.527.3788
10.00 - 21.00
Cash only

HOTPOT

Coriya
可利亞
3288 Pierce St., #A105
Richmond
510.524.8081
11.30 - 00.00
Mastercard, Visa

SHANGHAI

Shanghai Gourmet
3288 Pierce St., #B109
Richmond
510.526.8897
11.00 - 21.30
Mastercard, Visa

BAKERY

Sheng Kee Bakery
生記
3288 Pierce St.
Richmond
510.558.8807

TEASHOP

Ten Ren
天仁茗茶
3288 Pierce St., #C161
Richmond
510.526.3989

Appendix II: Restaurant Listings by Cuisine

GUANGDONG

SOUTH BAY/SILICON VALLEY

CUPERTINO

Joy Luck Place
醉香居
10911 N. Wolfe Rd.
Cupertino
408.255.6988
11.00 - 21.30
Mastercard, Visa

Silver Wing
銀翼飯店
10885 N. Wolfe Rd.
Cupertino
408.873.7228
11.00 - 21.00
Mastercard, Visa

MILPITAS

China First
中國第一
1741 N. Milpitas Blvd.
Milpitas
408.262.6226
11.00 - 21.30
Mastercard, Visa

Family Delight Café
家樂美食
662 Barber Ln.
Milpitas
408.943.8229
11.00 - 22.00
Cash only

New China Station B.B.Q.
Restaurant
新中國燒腊飯店
1828 N. Milpitas Blvd.
Milpitas
408.942.1686
10.30 - 21.30
Mastercard, Visa

New Hwong Kok
好旺角
1705 N. Milpitas Blvd.
Milpitas
408.263.8168
09.00 - 20.30
Cash only

Won Kee Seafood Restaurant
旺記海鮮酒家
206 Barber Ct.
Milpitas
408.955.9666
11.00 - 23.15
Mastercard, Visa

SAN JOSE

Chef Ming
天天漁港
1628 Hostetter Rd., #F, G
San Jose
408.436.8868
09.30 - 21.30
Mastercard, Visa

Loon Wah Restaurant
龍華餐館
1146 S. De Anza Blvd.
San Jose
408.257.8877
11.00 - 21.30
Mastercard, Visa

New China Station B.B.Q.
Restaurant
新中國燒腊飯店
1710 Tully Rd., #A
San Jose
408.531.8008
10.30 - 21.30
Mastercard, Visa

PENINSULA

MILLBRAE

Chueung Hing Restaurant
祥興燒腊小館
241-245 El Camino Real
Millbrae
650.652.3938
10.30 - 21.30
Mastercard, Visa

MOUNTAIN VIEW

Café Yulong
玉龍小館
743 W. Dana St.
Mountain View
650.960.1677
11.30 - 21.30, until 22.30 on
weekends
All credit cards

Fu Lam Mum Seafood
Restaurant
富臨門海鮮酒家
246 Castro St.
Mountain View
650.967.1689
11.00 - 00.00
All credit cards

Hangen Szechwan Restaurant
漢金
134 Castro St.
Mountain View
650.964.8881
11.00 - 21.30
Mastercard, Visa

Man Bo Duck Restaurant
萬寶鴨子樓
360 Castro St.
Mountain View
650.961.6635
11.00 - 00.00, until 01.00 on
weekends
All credit cards

PALO ALTO

Peking Duck Restaurant
鴨子閣
2310 El Camino Real
Palo Alto
650.856.3338
11.00 - 21.30
All credit cards

SAN FRANCISCO

CHINATOWN

ABC Bakery & Restaurant
ABC 餐廳餅家
650 Jackson St.
Chinatown
415.981.0803
08.00 - 23.00
Cash only

Chef Jia's
喜福家
925 Kearny St.
Chinatown
415.398.1626
11.30 - 22.00
Cash only

Chung King Restaurant
江南海鮮店
606 Jackson St.
Chinatown
415.986.3899
11.30 - 21.30
Mastercard, Visa

DPD Restaurant
中山小館
901 Kearny St.
Chinatown
415.398.4598
11.00 - 00.00, at 15.00 on Sunday
Cash only

Hon's Wun-Tun House (CA.)
Ltd.
洪記麵家
648 Kearny St.
Chinatown
415.433.3966
11.00 - 19.00, closed Sunday
Cash only

Little Garden Seafood Restaurant
新龍樓
750 Vallejo St.
Chinatown
415.788.2328
11.00 - 21.30
Mastercard, Visa

Louie's California Chinese
Cuisine
鑫源酒家
646 Washington St.
Chinatown
415.291.8038
17.00 - 22.00
All credit cards

Po Kee Restaurant
寶記粥麵飯店
1365 Stockton St.
Chinatown
415.788.7071
10.00 - 21.30
Cash only

R&G Lounge
嶺南小館
631 Kearny St.
Chinatown
415.982.7877
11.00 - 21.30
All credit cards

Silver Restaurant
銀輝燒臘海鮮
737 Washington St.
Chinatown
415.434.4998
11.00 - 00.00
All credit cards

Young's Café
寶馬餐廳
601 Kearny St.
Chinatown
415.397.3455
10.00 - 21.00, closed Sundays
All credit cards

RICHMOND DISTRICT

ABC Bakery & Restaurant
ABC 餐廳餅家
2500 Noriega St.
San Francisco (Richmond)
415.681.8800
07.00 - 03.00
Cash only

Family Fortune Restaurant
鑫培旺
5037 Geary Blvd.
San Francisco (Richmond)
415.221.8831
11.00 - 22.00
All credit cards

Kam's Restaurant
金華餐館
3620-24 Balboa St.
San Francisco (Richmond)
415.752.6355
11.00 - 21.00
All credit cards

Sun Wu Kong Restaurant
新滬江大飯店
5423 Geary Blvd.
San Francisco (Richmond)
415.876.2828
11.00 - 22.00

Tai San Restaurant
鴻圖小館
3420 Balboa St.
San Francisco (Richmond)
415.752.3362
11.00 - 21.30, closed Mondays
Cash only

OAKLAND/CONTRA COSTA

OAKLAND

Chef Lau's
佛笑樓海鮮館
301 8th St.
Oakland
510.835.3288
11.00 - 21.30, dinner only on
Tuesdays
All credit cards

Fortune Restaurant
福臨門酒家
940 Webster St.
Oakland
510.839.9697
11.00 - 02.30
Mastercard, Visa

Gold Medal Restaurant
金牌燒臘飯店
381 8th St.
Oakland
510.268.8484
09.00 - 21.00
Cash only

Gum Wah Restaurant
金華燒臘麵家
345 8th St.
Oakland
510.834.3103
08.00 - 19.00
Cash only

Happy Families Restaurant
天喜海鮮酒家
304 10th St.
Oakland
510.839.8871
09.00 - 21.30
Mastercard, Visa

Joy Luck Restaurant
敘樂酒家
327 8th St.
Oakland
510.832.4270
08.30 - 21.30
Mastercard, Visa

King Wah Restaurant
瓊華酒家
383 9th St.
Oakland
510.834.9769
11.00 - 21.00
Cash only

New Oakland Seafood
Restaurant
天倫海鮮酒家
307 10th St.
Oakland
510.893.3388
11.30 - 00.00
Mastercard, Visa

Sun Hing Meat Market
新興燒臘
386 8th St.
Oakland
510.836.1819
09.00 - 18.30
Cash only

Sun Hong Kong Restaurant
新香港酒家
389 8th St.
Oakland
510.465.1940
09.00 - 03.00
Cash only

Tin's Tea House Restaurant
醉瓊樓
701 Webster St.
Oakland
510.832.7661
09.00 - 21.30
All credit cards

Ying Kee Noodle House
英記麵家
373 8th St.
Oakland
510.251.1238
09.30 - 21.30
Cash only

Ying Kee Restaurant
英記食家
387 9th St.
Oakland
510.465.1888
09.30 - 21.30
Cash only

Yo Ho Restaurant
永和美食
337 8th St.
Oakland
510.268.0233
05.00 - 21.30
Mastercard, Visa

Yung Kee Restaurant
鏞記
888 Webster St.
Oakland
510.839.2010
09.00 - 02.00, until 03.00 on
weekends
Cash only

RICHMOND

Daimo Chinese Restaurant
地茂館香港美食
3288-A Pierce St.
Richmond
510.527.3888
09.00 - 03.00
Mastercard, Visa

SEAFOOD

SOUTH BAY/SILICON VALLEY

MILPITAS

ABC Seafood Restaurant
富豪皇宮海鮮酒家
768 Barber Ln.
Milpitas
408.435.8888
17.00 - 21.30
All credit cards

Fu Lam Moon Seafood
Restaurant
富臨門海鮮酒家
1678 N. Milpitas Blvd.
Milpitas
408.942.1888
17.00 - 00.00
All credit cards

Kowloon Restaurant
海運大酒家
24 S. Abbott Ave.
Milpitas
408.945.8888
17.00 - 21.30
All credit cards

Mayflower Restaurant
五月花酒家
428 Barber Ln.
Milpitas
408.922.2700
17.00 - 21.30
All credit cards

EAST BAY

NEWARK

Royal Garden Seafood
Restaurant
豪景魚翅海鮮酒家
35219 Newark Blvd.
Newark
510.494.8989
17.30 - 21.30
Mastercard, Visa

UNION CITY

China Villa Restaurant
馥林閣
34308 Alvarado Niles Rd.
Union City
510.475.8182
17.00 - 21.30
Mastercard, Visa

Lucky Palace Restaurant
新皇宮酒樓
34348 Alvarado Niles Rd.
Union City
510.489.8386
17.00 - 21.00
Mastercard, Visa

PENINSULA

DALY CITY

Koi Palace
鯉魚門海鮮茶寮
365 Gellert Blvd.
Daly City
650.992.9000
17.00 - 21.30
All credit cards

MILLBRAE

Fook Yuen Seafood Restaurant
馥苑海鮮酒家
195 El Camino Real
Millbrae
650.692.8600
17.30 - 21.30
All credit cards

Hong Kong Flower Lounge
香港香滿樓
51 Millbrae Ave.
Millbrae
650.692.6666
17.00 - 21.30
All credit cards

SAN FRANCISCO

CHINATOWN

Chinatown Restaurant
新杏香酒樓
8 Wentworth Alley
Chinatown
415.392.7958
10.00 - 22.00
All credit cards

Great Eastern Restaurant
迠賓閣
649 Jackson St.
Chinatown
415.986.2500
15.30 - 01.00
All credit cards

New Asia Chinese Restaurant
新亞洲大酒樓
772 Pacific Ave.
Chinatown
415.391.6666
17.00 - 21.00
Mastercard, Visa

Pearl City Seafood Restaurant
新珠城海鮮酒樓
641 Jackson St.
Chinatown
415.398.8383
15.00 - 22.00, until 23.00 on
weekends
Mastercard, Visa

Y. Ben House
會賓樓
835 Pacific Ave.
Chinatown
415.397.3168
16.00 - 21.00
Mastercard, Visa

RICHMOND DISTRICT

Lucky Fortune Seafood
Restaurant
新福滿樓海鮮酒樓
5715 Geary Blvd.
San Francisco (Richmond)
415.751.2888
15.00 - 23.00
Mastercard, Visa

Mayflower Restaurant
五月花酒家
6255 Geary Blvd.
San Francisco (Richmond)
415.387.8338
17.00 - 21.30
All credit cards

ELSEWHERE

Harbor Village Restaurant
海景假日翠亨沌茶寮
4 Embarcadero Center, Lobby
Level
San Francisco
415.781.7833
17.30 - 21.30
All credit cards

OAKLAND/CONTRA COSTA

OAKLAND

Restaurant Peony
牡丹閣海鮮酒家
388 9th St., #288
Oakland
510.286.8866
17.30 - 21.30
All credit cards

Jade Villa
翠苑
800 Broadway
Oakland
510.839.1688
09.30 - 21.00
Mastercard, Visa

Legendary Palace
燕喜樓
708 Franklin St.
Oakland
510.663.9188
17.00 - 23.00
Mastercard, Visa

Silver Dragon
銀龍酒家
835 Webster St.
Oakland
510.893.3748
11.30 - 20.30
All credit cards

RICHMOND

Pacific East Seafood Restaurant
東太海鮮酒樓
3288 Pierce St., #A118
Richmond
510.527.8968
11.00 - 03.00 until 04.00 on
weekends
Mastercard, Visa

Saigon Seafood Harbor
Restaurant
西貢漁港
3150 Pierce St.
Richmond
510.559.9388
11.00 - 23.00
Mastercard, Visa

DIM SUM/YUM CHA

SOUTH BAY/SILICON VALLEY

MILPITAS

ABC Seafood Restaurant
富豪皇宮海鮮酒家
768 Barber Ln.
Milpitas
408.435.8888
11.00 - 14.30, at 10.00 on
weekends
All credit cards

Fu Lam Moon Seafood
Restaurant
富臨門海鮮酒家
1678 N. Milpitas Blvd.
Milpitas
408.942.1888
11.00 - 14.30, at 10.00 on
weekends
All credit cards

Golden Island Chinese Cuisine
金島潮州酒家
282-286 Barber Ct.
Milpitas
408.383.9898
11.00 - 14.30, at 10.30 on
weekends
All credit cards

Kowloon Restaurant
海運大酒家
24 S. Abbott Ave.
Milpitas
408.945.8888
10.00 - 14.30
All credit cards

Mayflower Restaurant
五月花酒家
428 Barber Ln.
Milpitas
408.922.2700
11.00 - 14.30, at 10.00 on
weekends
All credit cards

EAST BAY

NEWARK

Royal Garden Seafood
Restaurant
豪景魚翅海鮮酒家
35219 Newark Blvd.
Newark
510.494.8989
11.00 - 14.30, at 10.00 on
weekends
Mastercard, Visa

UNION CITY

Lucky Palace Restaurant
新皇宮酒樓
34348 Alvarado Niles Rd.
Union City
510.489.8386
11.00 - 14.30, at 10.00 on
weekends
Mastercard, Visa

PENINSULA

DALY CITY

Koi Palace
鯉魚門海鮮茶寮
365 Gellert Blvd.
Daly City
650.992.9000
11.00 - 14.30, at 10.00 on
weekends
All credit cards

MILLBRAE

Fook Yuen Seafood Restaurant
馥苑海鮮家
195 El Camino Real
Millbrae
650.692.8600
11.00 - 14.30, at 10.00 on
weekends
All credit cards

Hong Kong Flower Lounge
香港香滿樓
51 Millbrae Ave.
Millbrae
650.692.6666
11.00 - 14.30, at 10.30 on
weekends
All credit cards

SAN FRANCISCO

CHINATOWN

Chinatown Restaurant
新杏香酒樓
8 Wentworth Alley
Chinatown
415.392.7958
10.00 - 15.00
All credit cards

Great Eastern Restaurant
迓賓閣
649 Jackson St.
Chinatown
415.986.2500
10.00 - 15.00
All credit cards

Louie's California Chinese
Cuisine
鑫源酒家
646 Washington St.
Chinatown
415.291.8038
10.00 - 15.00
All credit cards

New Asia Chinese Restaurant
新亞洲大酒樓
772 Pacific Ave.
Chinatown
415.391.6666
09.00 - 15.00
Mastercard, Visa

Pearl City Seafood Restaurant
新珠城海鮮酒樓
641 Jackson St.
Chinatown
415.398.8383
08.00 - 15.00
Mastercard, Visa

Y. Ben House
會賓樓
835 Pacific Ave.
Chinatown
415.397.3168
07.00 - 15.00
Mastercard, Visa

RICHMOND DISTRICT

Lucky Fortune Seafood
Restaurant
新福滿樓海鮮酒樓
5715 Geary Blvd.
San Francisco (Richmond)
415.751.2888
10.00 - 15.00
Mastercard, Visa

Ton Kiang
東江
5821 Geary Blvd.
San Francisco (Richmond)
415.387.8273
10.30 - 22.00
All credit cards

Mayflower Restaurant
五月花酒家
6255 Geary Blvd.
San Francisco (Richmond)
415.387.8338
11.00 - 14.30
All credit cards

ELSEWHERE

Harbor Village Restaurant
海景假日翠亨酕茶寮
4 Embarcadero Center, Lobby
Level
San Francisco
415.781.7833
11.00 - 14.30, at 10.30 on
weekends
All credit cards

Yank Sing
羊城茶室
101 Spear St. (One Rincon
Center)
San Francisco
415.957.9300
11.00 - 15.00 weekdays, 10.00
- 16.00 weekends
All credit cards

49 Stevenson St.
San Francisco
415.541.4949
11.00 - 15.00
All credit cards

OAKLAND/CONTRA COSTA

OAKLAND

Restaurant Peony
牡丹閣海鮮酒家
388 9th St., #288
Oakland
510.286.8866
11.00 - 15.00, at 10.00 on
weekends
All credit cards

Jade Villa
翠苑
800 Broadway
Oakland
510.839.1688
09.30 - 14.30
Mastercard, Visa

Joy Luck Restaurant
敘樂酒家
327 8th St.
Oakland
510.832.4270
08.30 - 14.30
Mastercard, Visa

Legendary Palace
燕喜樓
708 Franklin St.
Oakland
510.663.9188
10.00 - 14.30, at 09.00 on
weekends
Mastercard, Visa

Yo Ho Restaurant
永和美食
337 8th St.
Oakland
510.268.0233
09.00 - 14.30
Mastercard, Visa

RICHMOND

Pacific East Seafood Restaurant
東太海鮮酒樓
3288 Pierce St., #A118
Richmond
510.527.8968
11.00 - 15.00, until 16.00 on
weekends
Mastercard, Visa

Saigon Seafood Harbor
Restaurant
西貢漁港
3150 Pierce St.
Richmond
510.559.9388
11.00 - 15.00
Mastercard, Visa

HONGKONG-STYLE COFFEESHOP

SOUTH BAY/SILICON VALLEY

MILPITAS

Café Ophelia-Milpitas
芳苑岩燒西餐
516 Barber Ln.
Milpitas
408.943.1020
11.30 - 22.00, until 00.00 on
weekends
Mastercard, Visa

Chez Mayflower
竹皇美食中心
416 Barber Ln.
Milpitas
408.894.9171
11.00 - 22.30, until 00.00 on
weekends
Cash only

Top Café
尖峰菜餐館
650 Barber Ln.
Milpitas
408.262.3338
11.00 - 03.00
Cash only

SAN JOSE

Café 97
97 港式西餐
1701 Lundy Ave., #160
San Jose
408.573.8208
11.00 - 22.00
Cash only

Top Café
尖峰菜餐館
1075 S. De Anza Blvd.
San Jose
408.996.7797
11.00 - 03.00
Cash only

EAST BAY

FREMONT

Café Ophelia-Fremont
芳苑咖啡西餐
46801 Warm Springs Blvd.
Fremont
510.668.0998
11.00 - 00.00
Mastercard, Visa

Finchi Café
海中天
46875 Warm Springs Blvd.
Fremont
510.657.1488
11.00 - 00.00, at 10.00 on
weekends
Mastercard, Visa

NEWARK

Cousin Café
表哥茶餐廳
39193 Cedar Blvd.
Newark
510.713.9806
08.00 - 23.00, until 01.00 on
weekends
Cash only

SAN FRANCISCO

CHINATOWN

New Hollywood Bakery &
Restaurant
荷里活茶餐廳
652 Pacific Ave.
Chinatown
415.397.9919
07.00 - 18.00
Cash only

Sterling Ruby Restaurant
紅寶石餐廳
640 Jackson St.
Chinatown
415.982.0618
07.30 - 21.30
Mastercard, Visa

Washington Bakery & Restaurant
華盛頓茶餐廳
733 Washington St.
Chinatown
415.397.3232
07.30 - 21.00
Mastercard, Visa

OAKLAND/CONTRA COSTA

OAKLAND

D&A Café
文記茶餐廳
702 Webster St.
Oakland
510.839.6223
08.00 - 19.00
Cash only

RICHMOND

Orchid Bowl Café
澳門街
3288 Pierce St., #C156
Richmond
510.559.7888
11.00 - 22.00
Mastercard, Visa

> CHAOZHOU

SOUTH BAY/SILICON VALLEY

CUPERTINO

TK Noodle
20735 Stevens Creek Blvd.
Cupertino
408.257.9888
09.00 - 21.00
Cash only

MILPITAS

Golden Island Chinese Cuisine
金島潮州酒家
282-286 Barber Ct.
Milpitas
408.383.9898
17.00 - 22.00
All credit cards

New Tung Kee
新潮州中記麵家
481 E. Calaveras Blvd.
Milpitas
408.263.8288
09.00 - 21.00
Cash only

Penang Garden
278 Barber Ln.
Milpitas
408.321.8388
11.00 - 22.00
All credit cards

TK Noodle
1792 N. Milpitas Blvd.
Milpitas
408.935.9888
08.00 - 20.00

438 Barber Ln.
Milpitas
408.321.8889
09.00 - 21.00
Both locations cash only

SAN JOSE

Han Kee B.B.Q. Seafood
Restaurant
漢記潮州餐館
2017 Tully Rd.
San Jose
408.254.4665
08.00 - 22.00
Cash only

Kim Tar Restaurant
金塔粿條燒臘飯店
1698 Hostetter Rd., #J
San Jose
408.453.2006
10.30 - 00.00, at 09.30 on
weekends
Cash only

New Tung Kee
新潮州中記麵家
262 E. Santa Clara St.
San Jose
408.289.8688
09.00 - 21.00
Cash only

TK Noodle
1818 Tully Rd., #162B
San Jose
408.223.1688
08.00 - 20.00

261 E. William St.
San Jose
408.297.8888
08.00 - 20.00

336 N. Capitol Ave.
San Jose
408.937.1999
09.00 - 21.00

4068 Monterey Rd.
San Jose
408.365.1998
08.30 - 22.30

930 Story Rd.
San Jose
408.298.1688
08.00 - 20.00

975 McLaughlin Ave.
San Jose
408.286.9000
09.00 - 21.00

All locations cash only

SANTA CLARA

New Tung Kee
新潮州中記麵家
3577 El Camino Real
Santa Clara
408.261.8188
09.00 - 21.00
Cash only

> EAST BAY

FREMONT

New Tung Kee
新潮州中記麵家
39226 Argonaut Way
Fremont
510.795.2888
09.00 - 21.00
Cash only

NEWARK

New Tung Kee
新潮州中記麵家
35201 Newark Blvd.
Newark
510.818.1136
09.00 - 21.00
Cash only

TK Noodle
39029 Cedar Blvd.
Newark
510.494.9200
09.00 - 21.00
Cash only

> PENINSULA

DALY CITY

TK Noodle
6917 Mission St.
Daly City
650.994.8886
10.00 - 22.00
Cash only

MOUNTAIN VIEW

New Tung Kee
新潮州中記麵家
520 Showers Dr.
Mountain View
650.947.8888
09.00 - 21.00
Cash only

TK Noodle
357 Castro St.
Mountain View
650.605.1200
09.00 - 21.00
Cash only

SAN FRANCISCO

CHINATOWN

Capitol Kim Tar Restaurant
金塔粿條麵
758 Pacific Ave.
Chinatown
415.956.8533
09.00 - 21.00
Cash only

OAKLAND/CONTRA COSTA

OAKLAND

Vien Huong Restaurant
遠香蔬室
712 Franklin St.
Oakland
510.465.5938
07.30 - 19.00
Cash only

RICHMOND

VH Noodle House
遠香
3288 Pierce St., #B101
Richmond
510.527.3788
10.00 - 21.00
Cash only

HUNAN

EAST BAY

FREMONT

Chili Garden Restaurant
火宮殿
3213 Walnut Ave.
Fremont
510.792.8945
11.30 - 21.30
Mastercard, Visa

PENINSULA

MOUNTAIN VIEW

Hunan Chili
香辣軒
102 Castro St.
Mountain View
650.969.8968
11.00 - 21.30
All credit cards

SAN FRANCISCO

CHINATOWN

Brandy Ho's Hunan Food
何家湖南
217 Columbus Ave.
Chinatown
415.788.7527
11.00 - 23.30
All credit cards

Hunan Home's Restaurant
湖南又一村
622 Jackson St.
Chinatown
415.982.2844
11.30 - 21.30
All credit cards

HAKKA

PENINSULA

SAN MATEO

Hakka Restaurant
客人之家
137 E. 3rd Ave.
San Mateo
650.348.3559
11.00 - 21.00
Mastercard, Visa

SAN FRANCISCO

CHINATOWN

Mon Kiang Restaurant
梅江飯店
683 Broadway St.
Chinatown
415.421.2015
11.00 - 22.00
Mastercard, Visa

RICHMOND DISTRICT

Dragon River Restaurant
龍江飯店
5045 Geary Blvd.
San Francisco (Richmond)
415.387.8512
11.00 - 21.30
Mastercard, Visa

Ton Kiang
東江
5821 Geary Blvd.
San Francisco (Richmond)
415.387.8273
10.30 - 22.00
All credit cards

ISLAMIC-CHINESE

SOUTH BAY/SILICON VALLEY

MILPITAS

Darda Seafood Restaurant
清真一條龍
296 Barber Ct.
Milpitas
408.433.5199
11.00 - 21.30
Mastercard, Visa

SAN JOSE

Fatima Seafood Restaurant
清真馬家海鮮館
1132 De Anza Blvd., #A
San Jose
408.257.3893
11.00 - 21.30
Mastercard, Visa

Ma's Restaurant
清真馬家館
1715 Lundy Ave., #168
San Jose
408.437.2499
11.00 - 21.30
Mastercard, Visa

PENINSULA

SAN MATEO

Fatima Seafood Restaurant
清真馬家海鮮館
1208 S. El Camino Real
San Mateo
650.554.1818
11.00 - 21.30
Mastercard, Visa

SAN FRANCISCO

SUNSET DISTRICT

Old Mandarin Islamic Restaurant
老北京
3132 Vincente St.
San Francisco (Sunset)
415.564.3481
11.30 - 21.30, at 17.30 on
Tuesdays
Mastercard, Visa

DUMPLINGS & NOODLES

SOUTH BAY/SILICON VALLEY

MILPITAS

House of Noodles
老鄒麵館
690 Barber Ln.
Milpitas
408.321.8838
11.00 - 21.30
Cash only

EAST BAY

UNION CITY

Fortune Garden
一品香
1773 Decoto Rd.
Union City
510.487.9168
11.30 - 21.00, closed Tuesday
Cash only

PENINSULA

MOUNTAIN VIEW

Café Yulong
玉龍小館
743 W. Dana St.
Mountain View
650.960.1677
11.30 - 21.30, until 22.30 on
weekends
All credit cards

SAN MATEO

Sun Tung Restaurant
山東小館
153 S. B St.
San Mateo
650.342.5330
11.30 - 21.00, at 10.30 on
weekends. Closed Monday
Mastercard, Visa

SAN FRANCISCO

CHINATOWN

The Pot Sticker
熄京
150 Waverly Pl.
Chinatown
415.397.9985
11.00 - 22.00
Mastercard, Visa

OAKLAND/CONTRA COSTA

ALBANY

Chinese Village Restaurant
川味軒
1335 Solano Ave.
Albany
510.525.2285
11.00 - 22.00
All credit cards

OAKLAND

Shan Dong Mandarin Restaurant
山東館
328 10th St.
Oakland
510.839.2299
10.00 - 21.30
All credit cards

HOTPOT

SOUTH BAY/SILICON VALLEY

CUPERTINO

Kingswood Teppan Steak House
上林鐵板燒餐廳
10935 N. Wolfe Rd.
Cupertino
408.255.5928
11.30 - 22.30, until 00.00 on
weekends
Mastercard, Visa

MILPITAS

Café Ophelia-Milpitas
芳苑岩燒西餐
516 Barber Ln.
Milpitas
408.943.1020
11.30 - 22.00, until 00.00 on
weekends
Mastercard, Visa

Hot Pot City
可利亞火鍋城
500 Barber Ln.
Milpitas
408.428.0988
11.00 - 00.00, until 01.00 on
weekends
Mastercard, Visa

EAST BAY

FREMONT

Café Ophelia-Fremont
芳苑咖啡西餐
46801 Warm Springs Blvd.
Fremont
510.668.0998
17.30 - 00.00
Mastercard, Visa

NEWARK

Kingswood Teppan Steak House
上林鐵板燒餐廳
39055 Cedar Blvd.
Newark
11.30 - 22.30, until 00.00 on
weekends
Mastercard, Visa

Ninji's Mala Hot Pot Restaurant
寧記麻辣火鍋
6066 Mowry Ave.
Newark
510.792.2898
11.30 - 22.00
Mastercard, Visa

PENINSULA

DALY CITY

Koi Palace
鯉魚門海鮮茶寮
365 Gellert Blvd.
Daly City
650.992.9000
17.00 - 21.30
All credit cards

SAN FRANCISCO

SUNSET DISTRICT

Old Mandarin Islamic Restaurant
老北京
3132 Vincente St.
San Francisco (Sunset)
415.564.3481
11.30 - 21.30, at 17.30 on
Tuesdays
Mastercard, Visa

OAKLAND/CONTRA COSTA

ALBANY

Chinese Village Restaurant
川味軒
1335 Solano Ave.
Albany
510.525.2285
11.00 - 22.00
All credit cards

RICHMOND

Coriya
可利亞
3288 Pierce St., #A105
Richmond
510.524.8081
11.30 - 00.00
Mastercard, Visa

SICHUAN

SOUTH BAY/SILICON VALLEY

CUPERTINO

House of Sichuan
川蜀園
20007 Stevens Creek Blvd.
Cupertino
408.255.3328
11.30 - 21.30
Mastercard, Visa

MILPITAS

South Legend Sichuan
Restaurant
巴山蜀水
1720 N. Milpitas Blvd.
Milpitas
408.934.3970
11.00 - 21.00
Mastercard, Visa

EAST BAY

NEWARK

Su Gia Restaurant
大四川
35233 Newark Blvd.
Newark
510.742.8777
11.00 - 21.30
Mastercard, Visa

UNION CITY

Szechwan Home
渝榕人家
34396 Alvarado Niles Rd.
Union City
510.324.5000
11.00 - 22.00
All credit cards

SAN FRANCISCO

CHINATOWN

Sam Lok Restaurant
豆花飯莊
655 Jackson St.
Chinatown
415.981.8988
11.00 - 22.00
Mastercard, Visa

RICHMOND DISTRICT

Spices
辣妹子
291 6th Ave.
San Francisco (Richmond)
415.752.8885
11.00 - 21.45
Mastercard, Visa

294 8th Ave.
San Francisco (Richmond)
415.752.8884
11.00 - 21.45
Cash only

OAKLAND/CONTRA COSTA

ALBANY

Chinese Village Restaurant
川味軒
1335 Solano Ave.
Albany
510.525.2285
11.00 - 22.00
All credit cards

JIANGZHE

SOUTH BAY/SILICON VALLEY

CUPERTINO

A & J Restaurant
半畝園
10893 N. Wolfe Rd., #C
Cupertino
408.873.8298
11.00 - 21.00, at 08.00 on
weekends (for breakfast)
Cash only

Porridge Place
旺旺清粥
10869 N. Wolfe Rd.
Cupertino
408.873.8999
11.30 - 23.00
Cash only

Taipei Stone House Seafood
Restaurant
石家飯店
10877 N. Wolfe Rd.
Cupertino
408.255.8886
11.00 - 21.30
Mastercard, Visa

MILPITAS

Shang Hai Restaurant
江浙聚豐園
1708 N. Milpitas Blvd.
Milpitas
408.263.1868
11.00 - 21.00
Mastercard, Visa

SAN JOSE

A & J Restaurant
半畝園
1698 Hostetter Rd., #D
San Jose
408.441.8168
11.00 - 21.00, at 08.00 on
weekends (for breakfast
Cash only

Won Stew House
萬家香滷味
1715 Lundy Ave., #162
San Jose
408.392.9668
10.00 - 21.00
Cash only

EAST BAY

FREMONT

Shanghai Restaurant
三六九小館
46831 Warm Springs Blvd.
Fremont
510.668.0369
11.00 - 21.30, at 09.00 on
weekends
Mastercard, Visa

Won Stew House
萬家香滷味
46813 Warm Springs Blvd.
Fremont
510.683.0888
10.00 - 21.00
Mastercard, Visa

NEWARK

King's Garden Chinese Cuisine
敘香小館
39055 Cedar Blvd., #189
Newark
510.792.5866
11.00 - 22.30
Mastercard, Visa

PENINSULA

SAN BRUNO

Shanghai Town Restaurant
小江南
189 El Camino Real
San Bruno
650.615.9879
11.00 - 21.30
Mastercard, Visa

SAN FRANCISCO

CHINATOWN

Jai Yun
佳園
923 Pacific Ave.
Chinatown
415.981.7438
19.00 - 21.30, closed Thursday
Cash only

SHANGHAI

SOUTH BAY/SILICON VALLEY

MILPITAS

Ding Sheng Restaurant
上海鼎盛
686 Barber Ln.
Milpitas
408.943.8786
10.00 - 01.00
Mastercard, Visa

SAN FRANCISCO

CHINATOWN

Star Lunch
上海小吃
605 Jackson St.
Chinatown
415.788.6709
11.00 - 18.30, closes at 15.00
Mondays
Cash only

RICHMOND DISTRICT

Shanghai Dumpling Shop
上海飽餃店
3319 Balboa St.
San Francisco (Richmond)
415.387.2088
11.00 - 21.00, opens 10.00 on
weekends
Cash only

OAKLAND/CONTRA COSTA

OAKLAND

Shanghai Restaurant
上海小吃
930 Webster St.
Oakland
510.465.6878
11.00 - 22.00, until 01.00 on
weekends, lunch only Tuesdays
Mastercard, Visa

RICHMOND

Shanghai Gourmet
家家樂
3288 Pierce St., #B109
Richmond
510.526.8897
11.00 - 21.30
Mastercard, Visa

VEGETARIAN

SOUTH BAY/SILICON VALLEY

MILPITAS

Lu Lai Garden Vegetarian
Cuisine
如來素菜館
210 Barber Ct.
Milpitas
408.526.9888
10.30 - 21.15
Cash only

PENINSULA

MOUNTAIN VIEW

Garden Fresh Vegetarian
Restaurant
香根菜
1245 W. El Camino Real
Mountain View
650.961.7795
11.00 - 21.30, until 22.00 on
weekends
Mastercard, Visa

SAN FRANCISCO

CHINATOWN

Lucky Creation Vegetarian
如意齋素菜館
854 Washington St.
Chinatown
415.989.0818
11.00 - 21.30, closed Wednesday
Cash only

RICHMOND DISTRICT

Bok Choy Garden
喜香園素食館
1820 Clement St.
San Francisco (Richmond)
415.387.8111
11.00 - 21.00, closed Monday
Mastercard, Visa

ELSEWHERE

Golden Era Vegetarian
Restaurant
572 O'Farrell St.
San Francisco
415.673.3136
11.00 - 21.00, closed Tuesday
Mastercard, Visa

Hulu House Vegetarian
Restaurant
葫蘆鄉素食小吃
754 Kirkham St.
San Francisco
415.682.0826
11.00 - 21.00, closed Tuesday
Mastercard, Visa

Shangri-La Chinese Vegetarian
Restaurant
香格裡拉
2026 Irving St.
San Francisco
415.731.2548
11.30 - 21.00
Mastercard, Visa

OAKLAND/CONTRA COSTA

ALBANY

Mother Nature Vegetarian
Cuisine
大自然素食館
843 San Pablo Ave.
Albany
510.528.5388
11.30 - 21.00
Mastercard, Visa

BAKERY

SOUTH BAY/SILICON VALLEY

CUPERTINO

Sheng Kee Bakery
生記
10961 N. Wolfe Rd.
Cupertino
408.865.1900

10122 Brandley Dr.
Cupertino
408.255.9999

Sogo Bakery
10889 S. Blaney Ave.
Cupertino
408.253.0388

MILPITAS

Kee Wah Bakery
奇華餅家
1718 N. Milpitas Blvd.
Milpitas
408.956.8999

386 Barber Ln.
Milpitas
408.383.9288

Sheng Kee Bakery
生記
1842 N. Milpitas Blvd.
Milpitas
408.262.3388

290 Barber Ct.
Milpitas
408.428.9880

SAN JOSE

Sogo Bakery
1610 S. De Anza Blvd.
San Jose
408.861.0388

471 Saratoga Ave.
San Jose
408.554.0088

EAST BAY

FREMONT

Mary's Bakery
美力斯精緻烘焙
34370 Fremont Blvd.
Fremont
510.796.7875

Sogo Bakery
46875 Warm Springs Blvd.
Fremont
510.353.0988

UNION CITY

Sheng Kee Bakery
生記
34332 Alvarado Niles Rd.
Union City
510.477.9800

PENINSULA

MOUNTAIN VIEW

Hong Kong Bakery
香港餅家
210 Castro St.
Mountain View
650.578.0618

SAN MATEO

Sheng Kee Bakery
生記
2964 S. Norfolk Blvd.
San Mateo
650.341.8838

SAN FRANCISCO

CHINATOWN

ABC Bakery & Restaurant
ABC 餐廳餅家
650 Jackson St.
Chinatown
415.981.0803

Cheung Yuen Dim Sum
昌源點心
648 Pacific Ave.
Chinatown
415.834.1890

Louie's Dim Sum
新利園點心
1242 Stockton St.
Chinatown
415.989.8380

Washington Bakery & Restaurant
華盛頓茶餐廳
733 Washington St.
Chinatown
415.397.3232

Wing Sing
新永勝點心快餐
1125 Stockton St.
Chinatown
415.433.5571

ELSEWHERE

Sheng Kee Bakery
生記
1941 Irving St.
San Francisco
415.753.1111

OAKLAND/CONTRA COSTA

OAKLAND

ABC Bakery & Restaurant
ABC 餐廳餅家
388 9th St., #186
Oakland
510.836.2288

Sum Yee Bakery
新意糕點店
918 Webster St.
Oakland
510.268.8089

Sun Sing Pastry
新城糕點店
382 8th St.
Oakland
510.763.9228

Tao Yuen Pastry
桃園糕粉店
816 Franklin St.
Oakland
510.834.9200

RICHMOND

Sheng Kee Bakery
生記
3288 Pierce St.
Richmond
510.558.8807

SOUTH BAY/SILICON VALLEY

CUPERTINO

Ten Ren
天仁茗茶
10881 N. Wolfe Rd.
Cupertino
408.873.2038

MILPITAS

1732 N. Milpitas Blvd.
Milpitas
408.946.1118

EAST BAY

FREMONT

101 Tea Plantation
101 茶園
46859 Warm Springs Blvd.
Fremont
510.623.9606

NEWARK

Ten Ren
天仁茗茶
39115 Cedar Blvd.
Newark
510.713.9588

SAN FRANCISCO

CHINATOWN

Imperial Tea Court
裕隆茶莊
1411 Powell St.
Chinatown
415.788.6080
11.00 - 18.30, closed Tuesdays
All credit cards

Ferry Bldg.
San Francisco
415.544.9830
10.00 - 18.00, closed Mondays
All credit cards

Ten Ren
天仁茗茶
949 Grant Ave.
Chinatown
415.362.0656

OAKLAND/CONTRA COSTA

RICHMOND

Ten Ren
天仁茗茶
3288 Pierce St., #C161
Richmond
510.526.3989

Appendix III: Alphabetical Listings

101 Tea Plantation
101 茶園
46859 Warm Springs Blvd.
Fremont
510.623.9606
Teashop
Mastercard, Visa

A

A & J Restaurant
半畝園
10893 N. Wolfe Rd., #C
Cupertino
408.873.8298
Jiangzhe
11.00 - 21.00, at 08.00 on
weekends (for breakfast)
Cash only

1698 Hostetter Rd., #D
San Jose
408.441.8168
Jiangzhe
11.00 - 21.00, at 08.00 on
weekends (for breakfast)
Cash only

ABC Bakery & Restaurant
ABC 餐廳餅家
388 9th St., #186
Oakland
510.836.2288
Bakery
Cash only

ABC Bakery & Restaurant
ABC 餐廳餅家
650 Jackson St.
Chinatown
415.981.0803
Bakery
Guangdong
08.00 - 23.00
Cash only

ABC Bakery & Restaurant
ABC 餐廳餅家
2500 Noriega St.
San Francisco (Richmond)
415.681.8800
Guangdong
07.00 - 03.00
Cash only

ABC Seafood Restaurant
富豪皇宮海鮮酒家
768 Barber Ln.
Milpitas
408.435.8888
Dim sum/yum cha
11.00 - 14.30, at 10.00 on
weekends
Seafood
17.00 - 21.30
All credit cards

B

Bok Choy Garden
喜香園素食館
1820 Clement St.
San Francisco (Richmond)
415.387.8111
Vegetarian
11.00 - 21.00, closed Monday
Mastercard, Visa

Brandy Ho's Hunan Food
何家湖南
217 Columbus Ave.
Chinatown
415.788.7527
Hunan
11.00 - 23.30
All credit cards

C

Café 97
97 港式西餐
1701 Lundy Ave., #160
San Jose
408.573.8208
Coffeeshop
11.00 - 22.00
Cash only

Café Ophelia-Fremont
芳苑咖啡西餐
46801 Warm Springs Blvd.
Fremont
510.668.0998
Coffeeshop
11.00 - 00.00
Hotpots
17.30 - 00.00
Mastercard, Visa

Café Ophelia-Milpitas
芳苑岩燒西餐
516 Barber Ln.
Milpitas   408.943.1020
Coffeeshop
11.30 - 22.00, until 00.00 on
weekends
Hotpots
11.30 - 22.00, until 00.00 on
weekends
Mastercard, Visa

Café Yulong
玉龍小館
743 W. Dana St.
Mountain View
650.960.1677
Dumplings & Noodles
Guangdong
11.30 - 21.30, until 22.30 on
weekends
All credit cards

Capitol Kim Tar Restaurant
金塔粿條麵
758 Pacific Ave.
Chinatown
415.956.8533
Chaozhou
09.00 - 21.00
Cash only

Chef Jia's
喜福家
925 Kearny St.
Chinatown
415.398.1626
Guangdong
11.30 - 22.00
Cash only

Chef Lau's
佛笑樓海鮮館
301 8th St.
Oakland
510.835.3288
Guangdong
11.00 - 21.30, dinner only on
Tuesdays
All credit cards

Chef Ming
天天漁港
1628 Hostetter Rd., #F, G
San Jose
408.436.8868
Guangdong
09.30 - 21.30
Mastercard, Visa

Cheung Yuen Dim Sum
昌源點心
648 Pacific Ave.
Chinatown
415.834.1890
Bakery
07.00 - 18.00
Cash only

Chez Mayflower
竹皇美食中心
416 Barber Ln.
Milpitas
408.894.9171
Coffeeshop
11.00 - 22.30, until 00.00 on
weekends
Cash only

Chili Garden Restaurant
火宮殿
3213 Walnut Ave.
Fremont
510.792.8945
Hunan
11.30 - 21.30
Mastercard, Visa

China First
中國第一
1741 N. Milpitas Blvd.
Milpitas
408.262.6226
Guangdong
11.00 - 21.30
Mastercard, Visa

China Villa Restaurant
馥林閣
34308 Alvarado Niles Rd.
Union City
510.475.8182
Seafood
17.00 - 21.30
Mastercard, Visa

Chinatown Restaurant
新杏香酒樓
8 Wentworth Alley
Chinatown
415.392.7958
Dim sum/yum cha
10.00 - 15.00
Seafood
10.00 - 22.00
All credit cards

Chinese Village Restaurant
川味軒
1335 Solano Ave.
Albany
510.525.2285
Dumplings & Noodles
Sichuan
11.00 - 22.00
All credit cards

Chueung Hing Restaurant
祥興燒臘小館
241-245 El Camino Real
Millbrae
650.652.3938
Guangdong
10.30 - 21.30
Mastercard, Visa

Chung King Restaurant
江南海鮮店
606 Jackson St.
Chinatown
415.986.3899
Guangdong
11.30 - 21.30
Mastercard, Visa

Coriya
可利亞
3288 Pierce St., #A105
Richmond
510.524.8081
Hotpots
11.30 - 00.00
Mastercard, Visa

Cousin Café
表哥茶餐廳
39193 Cedar Blvd.
Newark
510.713.9806
Coffeeshop
08.00 - 23.00, until 01.00 on
weekends
Cash only

D

D&A Café
文記茶餐廳
702 Webster St.
Oakland
510.839.6223
Coffeeshop
08.00 - 19.00
Cash only

Daimo Chinese Restaurant
地茂館香港美食
3288-A Pierce St.
Richmond
510.527.3888
Guangdong
09.00 - 03.00
Mastercard, Visa

Darda Seafood Restaurant
清真一條龍
296 Barber Ct.
Milpitas
408.433.5199
Islamic
11.00 - 21.30
Mastercard, Visa

Ding Sheng Restaurant
上海鼎盛
686 Barber Ln.
Milpitas
408.943.8786
Shanghai
10.00 - 01.00
Mastercard, Visa

DPD Restaurant
中山小館
901 Kearny St.
Chinatown
415.398.4598
Guangdong
11.00 - 00.00, at 15.00 on Sunday
Cash only

Dragon River Restaurant
龍江飯店
5045 Geary Blvd.
San Francisco (Richmond)
415.387.8512
Hakka
11.00 - 21.30
Mastercard, Visa

F

Family Delight Café
家樂美食
662 Barber Ln.
Milpitas
408.943.8229
Guangdong
11.00 - 22.00
Cash only

Family Fortune Restaurant
鑫培旺
5037 Geary Blvd.
San Francisco (Richmond)
415.221.8831
Guangdong
11.00 - 22.00
All credit cards

Fatima Seafood Restaurant
清真馬家海鮮館
1132 De Anza Blvd., #A
San Jose
408.257.3893
Islamic
11.00 - 21.30
Mastercard, Visa

1208 S. El Camino Real
San Mateo
650.554.1818
Islamic
11.00 - 21.30
Mastercard, Visa

Finchi Café
海中天
46875 Warm Springs Blvd.
Fremont
510.657.1488
Coffeeshop
11.00 - 00.00, at 10.00 on
weekends
Mastercard, Visa

Fook Yuen Seafood Restaurant
馥苑海鮮酒家
195 El Camino Real
Millbrae
650.692.8600
Dim sum/yum cha
11.00 - 14.30, at 10.00 on
weekends
Seafood
17.30 - 21.30
All credit cards

Fortune Garden
一品香
1773 Decoto Rd.
Union City
510.487.9168
Dumplings & Noodles
11.30 - 21.00, closed Tuesday
Cash only

Fortune Restaurant
福臨門酒家
940 Webster St.
Oakland
510.839.9697
Guangzhou
11.00 - 02.30
Mastercard, Visa

Fu Lam Moon Seafood
Restaurant
富臨門海鮮酒家
1678 N. Milpitas Blvd.
Milpitas
408.942.1888
Dim sum/yum cha
11.00 - 14.30, at 10.00 on
weekends
Seafood
17.00 - 00.00
All credit cards

Fu Lam Mum Seafood
Restaurant
富臨門海鮮酒家
246 Castro St.
Mountain View
650.967.1689
Guangdong
11.00 - 00.00
All credit cards

G

Garden Fresh Vegetarian
Restaurant
香根菜
1245 W. El Camino Real
Mountain View
650.961.7795
Vegetarian
11.00 - 21.30, until 22.00 on
weekends
Mastercard, Visa

Gold Medal Restaurant
金牌燒腊飯店
381 8th St.
Oakland
510.268.8484
Guangdong
09.00 - 21.00
Cash only

Golden Era Vegetarian
Restaurant
572 O'Farrell St.
San Francisco
415.673.3136
Vegetarian
11.00 - 21.00, closed Tuesday
Mastercard, Visa

Golden Island Chinese Cuisine
金島潮州酒家
282-286 Barber Ct.
Milpitas
408.383.9898
Chaozhou
17.00 - 22.00
Dim sum/yum cha
11.00 - 14.30, at 10.30 on
weekends
All credit cards

Great Eastern Restaurant
連賓閣
649 Jackson St.
Chinatown
415.986.2500
Dim sum/yum cha
10.00 - 15.00
Seafood
15.30 - 01.00
All credit cards

Gum Wah Restaurant
金華燒腊麵家
345 8th St.
Oakland
510.834.3103
Guangdong
08.00 - 19.00
Cash only

H

Hakka Restaurant
客人之家
137 E. 3rd Ave.
San Mateo
650.348.3559
Hakka
11.00 - 21.00
Mastercard, Visa

Han Kee B.B.Q. Seafood
Restaurant
漢記潮州餐館
2017 Tully Rd.
San Jose
408.254.4665
Chaozhou
08.00 - 22.00
Cash only

Hangen Szechwan Restaurant
漢金
134 Castro St.
Mountain View
650.964.8881
Guangdong
11.00 - 21.30
Mastercard, Visa

Happy Families Restaurant
天喜海鮮酒家
304 10th St.
Oakland
510.839.8871
Guangdong
09.00 - 21.30
Mastercard, Visa

Harbor Village Restaurant
海景假日翠亨沌茶寮
4 Embarcadero Center, Lobby
Level
San Francisco
415.781.7833
Dim sum/yum cha
11.00 - 14.30, at 10.30 on
weekends
Seafood
17.30 - 21.30
All credit cards

Hong Kong Bakery
香港餅家
210 Castro St.
Mountain View
650.578.0618
Bakery

Hong Kong Flower Lounge
香港香滿樓
51 Millbrae Ave.
Millbrae
650.692.6666
Dim sum/yum cha
11.00 - 14.30, at 10.30 on
weekends
Seafood
17.00 - 21.30
All credit cards

Hon's Wun-Tun House (CA.)
Ltd.
洪記麵家
648 Kearny St.
Chinatown
415.433.3966
Guangdong
11.00 - 19.00, closed Sunday
Cash only

Hot Pot City
可利亞火鍋城
500 Barber Ln.
Milpitas
408.428.0988
Hotpots
11.00 - 00.00, until 01.00 on
weekends
Mastercard, Visa

House of Noodles
老鄰麵館
690 Barber Ln.
Milpitas
408.321.8838
Dumplings & Noodles
11.00 - 21.30
Cash only

House of Sichuan
川蜀園
20007 Stevens Creek Blvd.
Cupertino
408.255.3328
Sichuan
11.30 - 21.30
Mastercard, Visa

Hulu House Vegetarian
Restaurant
葫蘆鄉素食小吃
754 Kirkham St.
San Francisco
415.682.0826
Vegetarian
11.00 - 21.00, closed Tuesday
Mastercard, Visa

Hunan Chili
香辣軒
102 Castro St.
Mountain View
650.969.8968
Hunan
11.00 - 21.30
All credit cards

Hunan Home's Restaurant
湖南又一村
622 Jackson St.
Chinatown
415.982.2844
Hunan
11.30 - 21.30
All credit cards

I

Imperial Tea Court
裕隆茶莊
1411 Powell St.
Chinatown
415.788.6080
11.00 - 18.30, closed Tuesdays
All credit cards

Ferry Bldg.
San Francisco
415.544.9830
10.00 - 18.00, closed Mondays
Teashop
All credit cards

J

Jade Villa
翠苑
800 Broadway
Oakland
510.839.1688
Dim sum/yum cha
09.30 - 14.30
Seafood
09.30 - 21.00
Mastercard, Visa

Jai Yun
佳園
923 Pacific Ave.
Chinatown
415.981.7438
Jiangzhe
19.00 - 21.30, closed Thursday
Cash only

Joy Luck Place
醉香居
10911 N. Wolfe Rd.
Cupertino
408.255.6988
Guangdong
11.00 - 21.30
Mastercard, Visa

Joy Luck Restaurant
敘樂酒家
327 8th St.
Oakland
510.832.4270
Dim sum/yum cha
08.30 - 14.30
Guangdong
08.30 - 21.30
Mastercard, Visa

K

Kam's Restaurant
金華餐館
3620-24 Balboa St.
San Francisco (Richmond)
415.752.6355
Guangdong
11.00 - 21.00
All credit cards

Kee Wah Bakery
奇華餅家
1718 N. Milpitas Blvd.
Milpitas
408.956.8999

386 Barber Ln.
Milpitas
408.383.9288
Bakery

Kim Tar Restaurant
金塔粿條燒臘飯店
1698 Hostetter Rd., #J
San Jose
408.453.2006
Chaozhou
10.30 - 00.00, at 09.30 on
weekends
Cash only

King Wah Restaurant
瓊華酒家
383 9th St.
Oakland
510.834.9769
Guangdong
11.00 - 21.00
Cash only

King's Garden Chinese Cuisine
敍香小館
39055 Cedar Blvd., #189
Newark
510.792.5866
Jiangzhe
11.00 - 22.30
Mastercard, Visa

Kingswood Teppan Steak House
上林鐵板燒餐廳
10935 N. Wolfe Rd.
Cupertino
408.255.5928
11.30 - 22.30, until 00.00 on
weekends
Mastercard, Visa

39055 Cedar Blvd.
Newark
Opening September 2004
11.30 - 22.30, until 00.00 on
weekends
Hotpot
Mastercard, Visa

Koi Palace
鯉魚門海鮮茶寮
365 Gellert Blvd.
Daly City
650.992.9000
Dim sum/yum cha
11.00 - 14.30, at 10.00 on
weekends
Hotpot
17.00 - 21.30
Seafood
17.00 - 21.30
All credit cards

Kowloon Restaurant
海運大酒家
24 S. Abbott Ave.
Milpitas
408.945.8888
Dim sum/yum cha
10.00 - 14.30
Seafood
17.00 - 21.30
All credit cards

L

Legendary Palace
燕喜樓
708 Franklin St.
Oakland
510.663.9188
Dim sum/yum cha
10.00 - 14.30, at 09.00 on
weekends
Seafood
17.00 - 23.00
Mastercard, Visa

Little Garden Seafood Restaurant
新龍樓
750 Vallejo St.
Chinatown
415.788.2328
Guangdong
11.00 - 21.30
Mastercard, Visa

Loon Wah Restaurant
龍華餐館
1146 S. De Anza Blvd.
San Jose
408.257.8877
Guangdong
11.00 - 21.30
Mastercard, Visa

Louie's California Chinese
Cuisine
鑫源酒家
646 Washington St.
Chinatown
415.291.8038
Dim sum/yum cha
10.00 - 15.00
Guangdong
17.00 - 22.00
All credit cards

Louie's Dim Sum
新利園點心
1242 Stockton St.
Chinatown
415.989.8380
Bakery

Lu Lai Garden Vegetarian
Cuisine
如來素菜館
210 Barber Ct.
Milpitas
408.526.9888
Vegetarian
10.30 - 21.15
Cash only

Lucky Creation Vegetarian
如意齋素菜館
854 Washington St.
Chinatown
415.989.0818
Vegetarian
11.00 - 21.30, closed Wednesday
Cash only

Lucky Fortune Seafood
Restaurant
新福滿樓海鮮酒樓
5715 Geary Blvd.
San Francisco (Richmond)
415.751.2888
Dim sum/yum cha
10.00 - 15.00
Seafood
15.00 - 23.00
Mastercard, Visa

Lucky Palace Restaurant
新皇宮酒樓
34348 Alvarado Niles Rd.
Union City
510.489.8386
Dim sum/yum cha
11.00 - 14.30, at 10.00 on
weekends
Seafood
17.00 - 21.00
Mastercard, Visa

M

Man Bo Duck Restaurant
萬寶鴨子樓
360 Castro St.
Mountain View
650.961.6635
Guangdong
11.00 - 00.00, until 01.00 on
weekends
All credit cards

Mary's Bakery
美力斯精緻烘焙
34370 Fremont Blvd.
Fremont
510.796.7875
Bakery

Ma's Restaurant
清真馬家館
1715 Lundy Ave., #168
San Jose
408.437.2499
Islamic
11.00 - 21.30
Mastercard, Visa

Mayflower Restaurant
五月花酒家
428 Barber Ln.
Milpitas
408.922.2700
Dim sum/yum cha
11.00 - 14.30, at 10.00 on
weekends
Seafood
17.00 - 21.30
All credit cards

Mayflower Restaurant
五月花酒家
6255 Geary Blvd.
San Francisco (Richmond)
415.387.8338
Dim sum/yum cha
11.00 - 14.30
Seafood
17.00 - 21.30
All credit cards

Mon Kiang Restaurant
梅江飯店
683 Broadway St.
Chinatown
415.421.2015
Hakka
11.00 - 22.00
Mastercard, Visa

Mother Nature Vegetarian
Cuisine
大自然素食館
843 San Pablo Ave.
Albany
510.528.5388
Vegetarian
11.30 - 21.00
Mastercard, Visa

N

New Asia Chinese Restaurant
新亞洲大酒樓
772 Pacific Ave.
Chinatown
415.391.6666
Dim sum/yum cha
09.00 - 15.00
Seafood
17.00 - 21.00
Mastercard, Visa

New China Station B.B.Q.
Restaurant
新中國燒腊飯店
1828 N. Milpitas Blvd.
Milpitas
408.942.1686
Guangdong
10.30 - 21.30
Mastercard, Visa

1710 Tully Rd., #A
San Jose
408.531.8008
Guangdong
10.30 - 21.30
Mastercard, Visa

New Hollywood Bakery &
Restaurant
荷里活茶餐廳
652 Pacific Ave.
Chinatown
415.397.9919
Coffeeshop
07.00 - 18.00
Cash only

New Hwong Kok
好旺角
1705 N. Milpitas Blvd.
Milpitas
408.263.8168
Guangdong
09.00 - 20.30
Cash only

New Oakland Seafood
Restaurant
天倫海鮮酒家
307 10th St.
Oakland
510.893.3388
Guangdong
11.30 - 00.00
Mastercard, Visa

New Tung Kee
新潮州中記麵家
39226 Argonaut Way
Fremont
510.795.2888
09.00 - 21.00
Cash only

481 E. Calaveras Blvd.
Milpitas
408.263.8288
09.00 - 21.00
Cash only

520 Showers Dr.
Mountain View
650.947.8888
09.00 - 21.00
Cash only

35201 Newark Blvd.
Newark
510.818.1136
09.00 - 21.00
Cash only

262 E. Santa Clara St.
San Jose
408.289.8688
09.00 - 21.00
Cash only

3577 El Camino Real
Santa Clara
408.261.8188
09.00 - 21.00
Chaozhou
Cash only

Ninji's Mala Hot Pot Restaurant
寧記麻辣火鍋
6066 Mowry Ave.
Newark
510.792.2898
Hotpot
11.30 - 22.00
Mastercard, Visa

O

Old Mandarin Islamic Restaurant
老北京
3132 Vincente St.
San Francisco (Sunset)
415.564.3481
Hotpot
Islamic
11.30 - 21.30, at 17.30 on
Tuesdays
Mastercard, Visa

Orchid Bowl Café
澳門街
3288 Pierce St., #C156
Richmond
510.559.7888
Coffeeshop
11.00 - 22.00
Mastercard, Visa

P

Pacific East Seafood Restaurant
東太海鮮酒樓
3288 Pierce St., #A118
Richmond
510.527.8968
Dim sum/yum cha
11.00 - 15.00, until 16.00 on
weekends
Seafood
11.00 - 03.00 until 04.00 on
weekends
Mastercard, Visa

Pearl City Seafood Restaurant
新珠城海鮮酒樓
641 Jackson St.
Chinatown
415.398.8383
Dim sum/yum cha
08.00 - 15.00
Seafood
15.00 - 22.00, until 23.00 on
weekends
Mastercard, Visa

Peking Duck Restaurant
鴨子閣
2310 El Camino Real
Palo Alto
650.856.3338
Guangdong
11.00 - 21.30
All credit cards

Penang Garden
278 Barber Ln.
Milpitas
408.321.8388
Chaozhou
11.00 - 22.00
All credit cards

Po Kee Restaurant
寶記粥麵飯店
1365 Stockton St.
Chinatown
415.788.7071
Guangdong
10.00 - 21.30
Cash only

Porridge Place
旺旺清粥
10869 N. Wolfe Rd.
Cupertino
408.873.8999
Jiangzhe
11.30 - 23.00
Cash only

R

R&G Lounge
嶺南小館
631 Kearny St.
Chinatown
415.982.7877
Guangdong
11.00 - 21.30
All credit cards

Restaurant Peony
牡丹閣海鮮酒家
388 9th St., #288
Oakland
510.286.8866
Dim sum/yum cha
11.00 - 15.00, at 10.00 on
weekends
Seafood
17.30 - 21.30
All credit cards

Royal Garden Seafood
Restaurant
豪景魚翅海鮮酒家
35219 Newark Blvd.
Newark
510.494.8989
Dim sum/yum cha
11.00 - 14.30, at 10.00 on
weekends
Seafood
17.30 - 21.30
Mastercard, Visa

S

Saigon Seafood Harbor
Restaurant
西貢漁港
3150 Pierce St.
Richmond
510.559.9388
Dim sum/yum cha
11.00 - 15.00
Seafood
11.00 - 23.00
Mastercard, Visa

Sam Lok Restaurant
豆花飯莊
655 Jackson St.
Chinatown
415.981.8988
Sichuan
11.00 - 22.00
Mastercard, Visa

Shan Dong Mandarin Restaurant
山東館
328 10th St.
Oakland
510.839.2299
Dumplings & Noodles
10.00 - 21.30
All credit cards

Shang Hai Restaurant
江浙聚豐園
1708 N. Milpitas Blvd.
Milpitas
408.263.1868
Jiangzhe
11.00 - 21.00
Mastercard, Visa

Shanghai Dumpling Shop
上海飽飩店
3319 Balboa St.
San Francisco (Richmond)
415.387.2088
Shanghai
11.00 - 21.00, opens 10.00 on
weekends"
Cash only

Shanghai Gourmet
家家樂
3288 Pierce St., #B109
Richmond
510.526.8897
Shanghai
11.00 - 21.30
Mastercard, Visa

Shanghai Restaurant
三六九小館
46831 Warm Springs Blvd.
Fremont
510.668.0369
Jiangzhe
11.00 - 21.30, at 09.00 on
weekends
Mastercard, Visa

Shanghai Restaurant
上海小吃
930 Webster St.
Oakland
510.465.6878
Shanghai
11.00 - 22.00, until 01.00 on
weekends, lunch only Tuesdays
Mastercard, Visa

Shanghai Town Restaurant
小江南
189 El Camino Real
San Bruno
650.615.9879
Jiangzhe
11.00 - 21.30
Mastercard, Visa

Shangri-La Chinese Vegetarian
Restaurant
香格裡拉
2026 Irving St.
San Francisco
415.731.2548
Vegetarian
11.30 - 21.00
Mastercard, Visa

Sheng Kee Bakery
生記
10961 N. Wolfe Rd.
Cupertino
408.865.1900

10122 Brandley Dr.
Cupertino
408.255.9999

1842 N. Milpitas Blvd.
Milpitas
408.262.3388

290 Barber Ct.
Milpitas
408.428.9880

3288 Pierce St.
Richmond
510.558.8807

1941 Irving St.
San Francisco
415.753.1111

2964 S. Norfolk Blvd.
San Mateo
650.341.8838

34332 Alvarado Niles Rd.
Union City
510.477.9800
Bakery

Silver Dragon
銀龍酒家
835 Webster St.
Oakland
510.893.3748
Seafood
11.30 - 20.30
All credit cards

Silver Restaurant
銀輝燒臘海鮮
737 Washington St.
Chinatown
415.434.4998
Guangdong
11.00 - 00.00
All credit cards

Silver Wing
銀翼飯店
10885 N. Wolfe Rd.
Cupertino
408.873.7228
Guangdong
11.00 - 21.00
Mastercard, Visa

Sogo Bakery
10889 S. Blaney Ave.
Cupertino
408.253.0388

46875 Warm Springs Blvd.
Fremont
510.353.0988

1610 S. De Anza Blvd.
San Jose
408.861.0388

471 Saratoga Ave.
San Jose
408.554.0088
Bakery

South Legend Sichuan
Restaurant
巴山蜀水
1720 N. Milpitas Blvd.
Milpitas
408.934.3970
Sichuan
11.00 - 21.00
Mastercard, Visa

Spices
辣妹子
291 6th Ave.
San Francisco (Richmond)
415.752.8885
Sichuan
11.00 - 21.45
Mastercard, Visa

294 8th Ave.
San Francisco (Richmond)
415.752.8884
Sichuan
11.00 - 21.45
Cash only

Star Lunch
上海小吃
605 Jackson St.
Chinatown
415.788.6709
Shanghai
11.00 - 18.30, closes at 15.00
Mondays
Cash only

Sterling Ruby Restaurant
紅寶石餐廳
640 Jackson St.
Chinatown
415.982.0618
Coffeeshop
07.30 - 21.30
Mastercard, Visa

Su Gia Restaurant
大四川
35233 Newark Blvd.
Newark
510.742.8777
Sichuan
11.00 - 21.30
Mastercard, Visa

Sum Yee Bakery
新意糕點店
918 Webster St.
Oakland
510.268.8089
Bakery
07.00 - 19.00
Cash only

Sun Hing Meat Market
新興燒臘
386 8th St.
Oakland
510.836.1819
Guangdong
09.00 - 18.30
Cash only

Sun Hong Kong Restaurant
新香港酒家
389 8th St.
Oakland
510.465.1940
Guangdong
09.00 - 03.00
Cash only

Sun Sing Pastry
新城糕點店
382 8th St.
Oakland
510.763.9228
Bakery

Sun Tung Restaurant
山東小館
153 S. B St.
San Mateo
650.342.5330
Dumplings & Noodles
11.30 - 21.00, at 10.30 on
weekends. Closed Monday
Mastercard, Visa

Sun Wu Kong Restaurant
新滬江大飯店
5423 Geary Blvd.
San Francisco (Richmond)
415.876.2828
Guangdong
11.00 - 22.00

Szechwan Home
渝榕人家
34396 Alvarado Niles Rd.
Union City
510.324.5000
Sichuan
11.00 - 22.00
All credit cards

T

Tai San Restaurant
鴻圖小館
3420 Balboa St.
San Francisco (Richmond)
415.752.3362
Guangdong
11.00 - 21.30, closed Mondays
Cash only

Taipei Stone House Seafood
Restaurant
石家飯店
10877 N. Wolfe Rd.
Cupertino
408.255.8886
Jiangzhe
11.00 - 21.30
Mastercard, Visa

Tao Yuen Pastry
桃園糕粉店
816 Franklin St.
Oakland
510.834.9200
Bakery

Ten Ren
天仁茗茶
10881 N. Wolfe Rd.
Cupertino
408.873.2038

1732 N. Milpitas Blvd.
Milpitas
408.946.1118

39115 Cedar Blvd.
Newark
510.713.9588

3288 Pierce St., #C161
Richmond
510.526.3989

949 Grant Ave.
Chinatown
415.362.0656
Teashop

The Pot Sticker
燌京
150 Waverly Pl.
Chinatown
415.397.9985
Dumplings & Noodles
11.00 - 22.00
Mastercard, Visa

Tin's Tea House Restaurant
醉瓊樓
701 Webster St.
Oakland
510.832.7661
Guangdong
09.00 - 21.30
All credit cards

TK Noodle
20735 Stevens Creek Blvd.
Cupertino
408.257.9888
09.00 - 21.00

6917 Mission St.
Daly City
650.994.8886
10.00 - 22.00

1792 N. Milpitas Blvd.
Milpitas
408.935.9888
08.00 - 20.00

438 Barber Ln.
Milpitas
408.321.8889
09.00 - 21.00

357 Castro St.
Mountain View
650.605.1200
09.00 - 21.00

39029 Cedar Blvd.
Newark
510.494.9200
09.00 - 21.00

1818 Tully Rd., #162B
San Jose
408.223.1688
08.00 - 20.00

261 E. William St.
San Jose
408.297.8888
08.00 - 20.00

336 N. Capitol Ave.
San Jose
408.937.1999
09.00 - 21.00

4068 Monterey Rd.
San Jose
408.365.1998
08.30 - 22.30

930 Story Rd.
San Jose
408.298.1688
08.00 - 20.00

975 McLaughlin Ave.
San Jose
408.286.9000
09.00 - 21.00
Chaozhou
All locations cash only

Ton Kiang
東江
5821 Geary Blvd.
San Francisco (Richmond)
415.387.8273
Dim sum/yum cha
10.30 - 22.00
Hakka
10.30 - 22.00
All credit cards

Top Café
尖峰菜餐館
650 Barber Ln.
Milpitas
408.262.3338
Coffeeshop
11.00 - 03.00
Cash only

Top Café
尖峰菜餐館
1075 S. De Anza Blvd.
San Jose
408.996.7797
Coffeeshop
11.00 - 03.00
Cash only

V

VH Noodle House
遠香
3288 Pierce St., #B101
Richmond
510.527.3788
Chaozhou
10.00 - 21.00
Cash only

Vien Huong Restaurant
遠香薈室
712 Franklin St.
Oakland
510.465.5938
Chaozhou
07.30 - 19.00
Cash only

W

Washington Bakery & Restaurant
華盛頓茶餐廳
733 Washington St.
Chinatown
415.397.3232
Coffeeshop
07.30 - 21.00
Mastercard, Visa

Wing Sing
新永勝點心快餐
1125 Stockton St.
Chinatown
415.433.5571
Bakery

Won Kee Seafood Restaurant
旺記海鮮酒家
206 Barber Ct.
Milpitas
408.955.9666
Guangdong
11.00 - 23.15
Mastercard, Visa

Won Stew House
萬家香滷味
46813 Warm Springs Blvd.
Fremont
510.683.0888
10.00 - 21.00
Mastercard, Visa

1715 Lundy Ave., #162
San Jose
408.392.9668
10.00 - 21.00
Jiangzhe
Cash only

Y

Y. Ben House
會賓樓
835 Pacific Ave.
Chinatown
415.397.3168
Dim sum/yum cha
07.00 - 15.00
Seafood
16.00 - 21.00
Mastercard, Visa

Yank Sing
羊城茶室
101 Spear St. (One Rincon
Center)
San Francisco
415.957.9300
11.00 - 15.00 weekdays, 10.00
- 16.00 weekends

49 Stevenson St.
San Francisco
415.541.4949
11.00 - 15.00
Dim sum/yum cha
All credit cards

Ying Kee Noodle House
英記麵家
373 8th St.
Oakland
510.251.1238
Guangdong
09.30 - 21.30
Cash only

Yo Ho Restaurant
永和美食
337 8th St.
Oakland
510.268.0233
Dim sum/yum cha
09.00 - 14.30
Guangdong
05.00 - 21.30
Mastercard, Visa

Young's Café
寶馬餐廳
601 Kearny St.
Chinatown
415.397.3455
Guangdong
10.00 - 21.00, closed Sundays
All credit cards

Yung Kee Restaurant
鏞記
888 Webster St.
Oakland
510.839.2010
Guangdong
09.00 - 02.00, until 03.00 on
weekends
Cash only

GLOSSARY

A

ahimsa
Buddhist belief of non-injury to animals and humans.

airpot
A cooking vessel for herbal medicines famous in Yunnan province.

B

bahn loc
Coarse rice noodles popular in Vietnam.

baozi
Round dumplings that are steamed or grilled.

biluochun
Famous green tea grown near Suzhou in eastern China.

boba
Pellet-size starch balls made from yams, used in beverages.

C

candied flossing
Shandong dessert-making technique.

cellophane noodles
Thin, clear noodles made from green (mung) bean flour.

Chaozhou
City in eastern Guangdong province; site of heavy Chinese immigration to Southeast Asia in mid-1800s.

charsui
Guangdong barbecue method by hanging meats on hooks over open flames.

Chengdu
Provincial capital of Sichuan province.

Chongqing
Industrial city in eastern Sichuan.

chong fun
Rice noodles wrapped into sausage-like shapes.

chow mein
Pan-fried egg noodles.

Chu Hou sauce
Cooking condiment made of equal portions of plum sauce and sweet bean paste.

congee
Thin rice cereal flavored with a variety of ingredients.

D

dabing
Big pancake, a staple of Islamic-Chinese cuisine.

dalu mian
Shandong noodles served in a starchy soup.

Dongjiang
East River" of Guangdong province; site of many Hakka communities.

douhua
Soymilk gelatin made solid by addition of edible plaster.

Duanwujie
Chinese holiday in celebration of Qu Yuan, a famous poet.

E

earthenware hotpot
A cooking and serving vessel made of clay, used for making stews.

egg custard tart
A pastry with an egg custard baked into a flaky pie crust.

F

fermented rice mash
Sweet condiment of fermented rice with a slight alcohol content.

finning
A practice of harvesting shark's fins at sea.

fish-flavor
A famous Sichuan technique for preparing meats and vegetables.

fun
"Rice noodles, to a Guangdong person.

fun gor
A Chaozhou-style dim sum dumpling similar to jiaozi, made of rice flour."

Fuzhou
A port city in northeastern Fuzhou province; also its provincial capital.

G

gluten
Natural proteins found in wheat and other grains.

H

halal
Foods that meet Islamic dietary laws.

Hangzhou
Provincial capital of Zhejiang province.

haram
Not halal according to the Koran; unsuitable for the Muslim diet.

haute cuisine
Creative or inventive dishes that challenge old traditional views.

hawker
Street vendors.

hecai
Chop suey, to a northern Chinese.

huajiao
Sichuan peppercorns, a vital condiment of Sichuan cuisine.

Hui
Ethnic minority of Chinese Muslims with Arabic origins.

hu tieu
Chaozhou-style rice noodles.

I

Islamic-Chinese
Describes the traditions (including the food) of the Huis.

J

jasmine
Fragrant flower used to scent green and oolong teas.

Jiangzhe
A prosperous province along the Yangtze in eastern China.

Jianzhong
Saltpeter zhongzi, a fillingless rice ball treated with saltpeter.

jiaozi
Oblong-shaped dumplings, most often boiled.

K

kaofu
Deep-fried wheat gluten, used as a meat substitute.

kourou
Steamed dish of sliced pork belly.

L

larou
Hunan-style preserved meats.

lo mein
Guangdong-style noodle dish with
the soup served separately.

M

malaguo
Sichuan-style hotpot with a numbing-
hot cooking broth as its base.

mantou
Steamed lump of flour, or steamed
bread.

mentaiko
Smoked cod roe, reddish in color;
used throughout Japanese cooking.

milk soup
Shandong-style soup made by boiling
bones over high heat.

mochi
Japanese-style rice balls.

N

niang
Hakka-style dish of stuffed
vegetables with meats.

Ningbo
A port city in Zhejiang province.

O

oolong
Partially-oxidized tea, grown mostly
in Fujian province and Taiwan.

orecchiétte
Ear-shaped pasta popular in Italy.

osmanthus
Fragrant flower with leathery green
leaves. Used as a condiment.

P

pinyin
The standard Romanized writing
system for Chinese, based on
Mandarin pronunciations.

potsticker
Pan-fried jiaozi.

pouchong
Oolong tea that only undergoes ten
percent oxidation.

pu-er
110% oxidized black tea popular in
Guangdong province.

Q

Quanjude
A popular Beijing duck franchise
based in mainland China.

Qu Yuan
(340-278 B.C) A famous poet from
the Warring States Period.

S

saltpeter
Potassium Nitrate, a compound used
in fireworks and curing meats.

shaobing
Small pancake eaten for breakfast or
as bread in northern China.

shenjianbao
Pan-fried small soupy baozi.

shuangdong
The combination of bamboo shoots
and mushrooms.

sriracha
A chili pepper native of Southeast
Asia.

T

tamarind
Fruit pod used to create tangy flavors
in dishes.

tapioca
Whitish starch used widely in
cooking throughout the world, mostly
as thickener.

ti kuan yin
Oolong tea that undergoes more
oxidation than other types.

W

wowotou
Northern Chinese bread resembling
corn cake.

X

xiaolongbao
Small soupy baozi steamed in
individual-size portions of eight to
ten.

XO sauce
A spicy Hongkong-style seafood
condiment of dried scallops.

Y

yanwan
Fuzhou meat balls resembling
wontons.

youtiao
Deep-fried flour dough treated with
saltpeter.

yuanyang
Any combination of two things,
usually complimentary.

yuanyangguo
A divided hotpot capable of holding
two types of cooking broths.

Z

zhacai
Sichuan specialty of pickled mustard
tubers.

zhaicai
Chinese vegetarian cuisine inspired
by the food of the monasteries.

zhongzi
Rice balls wrapped in bamboo leaves,
eaten on Duanwujie.

Oakland Chinatown